EVEN UNTO DEATH

EVEN
UNTO
DEATH

THE HEROIC WITNESS OF THE
SIXTEENTH-CENTURY
ANABAPTISTS

BY JOHN CHRISTIAN WENGER

JOHN KNOX PRESS
Richmond, Virginia

Library of Congress Catalog Card Number: 61-15763

© M. E. Bratcher 1961
Printed in the United States of America
7837

FOREWORD

✠

In Ephesians 3 Paul prays that we "may have power to comprehend with all the saints what is the breadth and length and height and depth and to know the love of Christ which surpasses knowledge." The love of Christ, we have learned to recognize, is not confined or exhibited in all of its richness in any individual, group, or denomination, in any single land, or in any particular age. If we are to know the love of Christ in fullest measure, if we are to grow in our knowledge as we ought, we must seek to comprehend with all the saints, with *all* the saints, with those of every age, and with those in every denominational group.

It is only in recent years that the body of Christ as a whole has come to know and appreciate the witness, in word and deed, "even unto death," of one of the most important Reformation movements, that of the Anabaptists, from whom our modern Mennonites, Amish, and Hutterians have come by direct descent, and our various Baptist bodies, more indirectly. Harrowed unmercifully, persecuted by Roman Catholics, Lutherans, and Reformed, the Anabaptists were reduced to a numerically insignificant minority in Europe, yet some of the ideas for which they stood have become the common possession and the glory of a large part of Christendom, while others remain to challenge us to discipleship at a deeper level.

Much has been done in recent years, and not only by Mennonite historians, to correct the misunderstandings—and perversions—which were transmitted regarding Anabaptist beliefs. To this growing literature Professor Wenger has made a distinct contribution. He has given us case studies of typical Anabaptist martyrs, and has quoted copiously from Anabaptist writings to clarify the Anabaptist theology. His book is one of the best introductions now available to the movement as a whole; it adds concrete detail from the original sources to what has been previously written. And in line with Paul's prayer it will serve as an aid to that fuller comprehension of God's love in Christ which displayed its power in a multitude of humble men in the 16th century, and from which we need to learn in the latter half of the 20th century.

ERNEST TRICE THOMPSON

PREFACE

✠

It has taken four centuries to overcome the distorted and biased portrait of the Anabaptists drawn by their opponents, but it has finally been accomplished. We now know how devoutly these *Täufer,* as they were called in German, sought to follow Christ, how earnestly they loved God's Word and tried to obey it, how seriously they clung to the principle of freedom of conscience, how profoundly they opposed the principle of a state church, how vigorously they objected to binding salvation to ceremonies, and how eagerly they attempted the evangelization of Europe. They had a theology and ethic which were well thought out, and which they were eager to share with all men, princes and peasants alike. But they were often told to dispute with the hangman, and were thrown into prison, whence they were led out to martyrdom. Organized Christendom called upon the state to root out these "heretics" who dared to challenge such tenets of Christendom as the established church, the swearing of oaths, and infant baptism—not to mention capital punishment and warfare.

The fairest approach to the beliefs and program of a religious group is that of mastering the primary sources of the group itself. We now recognize that we could never understand the genius of Lutheranism or the program of Luther himself by swallowing the polemical literature of his sixteenth-century opponents; likewise with Wesley and his valiant effort to revive the eighteenth-century Church of England. This book is an effort to interpret the sixteenth-century Anabaptists in terms of their own testimonies in court, their letters, tracts, books, and confessions of faith. Even the Mennonites, who are the lineal descendants of the original Swiss and Dutch Anabaptists, have only a partial knowledge of the richness of their spiritual heritage.

Very little was done prior to the nineteenth century by way of a scientific analysis and interpretation of Anabaptism. Even today many historians are still copying the diatribes against the movement manufactured by the vigorous, but careless, polemicists of the sixteenth century. Few modern writers of course would relish the Jesuit booklet of 1603, by Christoph Andreas Fischer, *Concerning the Accursed Origin and Ungodly Doctrine of the Anabaptists, and a Thorough Refutation Thereof.*

Five publications have reversed the unfavorable judgment of past historians on Anabaptism. (1) In the Netherlands, except for five years, the *Doopsgezinde Bijdragen* (Mennonite Contributions) appeared annually from 1861 to 1919, and contained a large number of scholarly articles on Dutch Anabaptism and Mennonitism. (2) In 1913 two German Mennonite scholars, Christian Hege and Christian Neff, began the publication of a four-volume *Mennonitisches Lexikon* (Mennonite Lexicon), which is even today not yet complete. Hege and Neff kept abreast of the latest scholarship and made use of archival materials in their creative reinterpretations of Anabaptism. (3) Since 1927 the Mennonite Historical Society, Goshen College, Goshen, Indiana, has been issuing under the able leadership of Editor Harold S. Bender, *The Mennonite Quarterly Review*, which is now the leading journal in the field. (4) Since 1930 the European Society for Reformation History has been issuing a series of volumes containing Anabaptist source materials, commonly called *Täuferakten* (Anabaptist documents), under the title, *Quellen zur Geschichte der Täufer* (Sources on the History of the Anabaptists). (5) The fruit of all this research was finally gathered together in four solid volumes, *The Mennonite Encyclopedia* (Scottdale, Pennsylvania: Mennonite Publishing House, 1955-59), under the leadership of Harold S. Bender and a strong editorial staff. There is no longer any excuse for ignoring the evidence as to the faith and life of the Anabaptists.

Strangely enough, historians have generally overlooked a huge book of over twelve hundred pages which had been published in the Netherlands in 1660, and which contains an enormous amount of archival material on the Anabaptists of the Low Countries. This book, the *Martyrs Mirror*, by T. J. van Braght, names 613 martyrs from the Netherlands and Belgium, and 190 others from various parts of Europe, as well as describing a large number of martyrdoms of unnamed persons: men, women, and youths. This martyrology the Mennonites carried with them from one country to another in their centuries-long search for religious toleration and freedom.

It is hoped that a brief summary of the faith of the Anabaptists and their violent suppression, which almost annihilated them, will contribute to a fuller understanding of the glorious Reformation of the sixteenth century. It is not anticipated that large numbers of twentieth-century Christians will adopt *in toto* the ethic and theology of the Anabaptists; yet it is possible that many earnest believers today will ponder deeply the Anabaptists' conviction that the followers of the Prince of Peace ought to operate only on the principles of love and good will. Surely the hour has struck for Christendom to learn the folly of warfare, especially of nuclear destruction. The principle of the free church has already been accepted by all American religious bodies, indeed by much of the occident. The doctrine of believer's baptism is today espoused by not only the great Baptist fellowship around the globe, but also by so influential a theologian as Professor Karl Barth of Basle. There is something remarkably modern about the Anabaptist principle of voluntarism in faith, and the insistence that to be a Christian calls for an earnest discipleship to Jesus Christ in life. Freedom of conscience is today cherished as one of the most precious principles of our Western heritage.

Readers will, of course, have differing opinions regarding the degree to which Conrad Grebel, the founder of Anabaptism, was right or wrong theologically. But all readers will admire a man who loved the truth above family, home, and church, and who was prepared to lay down his life rather than to compromise with error. "I will bear testimony to the truth," asserted Grebel in 1525, "with the spoiling of my goods, yea, of my home, which is all I have. I will testify to the truth with imprisonments, with confiscations, with death." Grebel died as a courageous and determined Christian pilgrim of twenty-eight of the plague at the Swiss town of Maienfeld a little over a year after he made this declaration. Imprisonment and bonds and illness had taken their toll, but his spirit was still free, and the truth for which he gave his life could not be fettered. Hübmaier was right: "Divine truth is immortal."

It is a pleasure to express my gratitude to Dr. Ernest Trice Thompson, Professor of Church History in Union Theological Seminary, Richmond, Virginia, for his kind consent to write an introduction to this book. I am also deeply grateful to the editors of John Knox Press for many fine suggestions for the improvement of the manuscript. For the defects which remain, I alone am responsible. I also wish to express my appreciation to Mr. Ellrose D. Zook, Executive Editor of Herald Press, for permission to quote from *The Complete Writings of Menno Simons,* copyright 1956 by Mennonite Publishing House, Scottdale, Pennsylvania.

Finally, a word of concern must be expressed. It is my sincere hope that the story told in this volume will add to contemporary appreciation for the Reformation without in any sense inciting ill will toward any twentieth-century Christian denomination. The Anabaptists were pioneers for religious toleration in an age when their cries went unheeded. May the great gains which have been made in the area of the basic freedoms never be lost, but rather may they continue to spread around the globe.

This book is sent forth with the conviction that Christendom will read with profit of the faith and life of the persecuted Anabaptists of the sixteenth century. May Jesus Christ, the great Head of the church, be pleased to use this witness for his glory.

J. C. WENGER
Goshen College Biblical Seminary
Goshen, Indiana

CONTENTS

✠

Divine truth is immortal. And although it may long be bound, scourged, crowned [with thorns], crucified, and laid in the grave, yet on the third day it will rise again victoriously, and will reign and triumph eternally.

BALTHASAR HÜBMAIER
Martyred March 10, 1528

EVEN UNTO DEATH

I

THE SWISS CRADLE
OF ANABAPTISM

✠

For many years the real origin of Anabaptism was not known. It has now been demonstrated beyond doubt that the true cradle was Zurich, Switzerland, and the chief founder was Conrad Grebel. The definitive biography of Grebel[1] was published in the year 1950, and this monograph, together with the Swiss archival materials on Anabaptism which apeared two years later,[2] are decisive that the original *Täufer* ("Baptists") were the 1525 dissenters from Ulrich Zwingli, founder of the German Swiss reformation. Grebel himself, son of a prominent patrician family of the city and canton, was led to evangelical faith by Zwingli; and for a number of years he looked to Zwingli as his spiritual father, and as the hope of the coming Swiss evangelical church.

Grebel had a short career. Born about the year 1498 he was the son of the iron merchant Jacob Grebel and his wife Dorothea Fries Grebel. From the age of about eight until he was sixteen Grebel studied in the *Carolina,* a Latin school in Zurich named for Carl the Great (Charlemagne). In the fall of 1514 Conrad matriculated in the University of Basle and studied there for one year. A year later he enrolled in the University of Vienna where his father had secured for him a royal stipend. He remained at Vienna for three years and became an accomplished humanist scholar. In 1518 he transferred to the University of Paris where he also enjoyed a royal stipend, again arranged by his father. After two years in Paris he returned home, although at that point he still intended to resume his academic training—

this time at the University of Pisa where he was to enjoy a papal grant. But his plan to study at Pisa never materialized, and he failed ever to earn a doctorate. Grebel was not outstanding as a Christian during his university days; he was far more an average sample of the careless living characteristic of the university youth of the period.

Grebel had other troubles. Not only was he unsuccessful in completing his doctoral studies, he also began to suffer with ill health, and his parents were unhappy with his life in general. Father and son were especially critical of each other. The somewhat impudent son could write to Vadian (Dr. Joachim von Watt), married to Martha Grebel, Conrad's sister: "Sniff onions, and go hang." Conrad complained bitterly that his father had never taught him how to use money, and he demonstrated rather well the truth of his complaint. Thus the unhappy youth returned to Zurich from Paris in 1520. The climax of the tension with his parents came in another form of "trouble"—that is, trouble for the parents but ecstasy for young Conrad. In 1521 he fell in love with a Zurich girl with all the intensity of youth. Unfortunately she did not spring from a patrician family like the Grebels, and her name has come down to us only as Barbara. The Grebels were determined to crush the affair, and Conrad was just as determined to have his *Holokosme* ("all the world") as he called her. On February 6, 1522, Conrad courageously married her, despite violent parental objection. Three children graced their home: Theophilus (born 1522), who died unmarried; Joshua (born 1523), who married Catherine Steiner, and whose descendants, the Von Grebels, still live in Zurich (Pastor Hans Rudolf von Grebel is now pastor of Zwingli's Great Minster in the City); and Rachel (born 1525), who died as an infant.

Grebel's conversion to a genuine obedience to Christ, to a real Christian life, and to an evangelical faith came the spring or summer of 1522, and the pastor responsible for the conversion was Zwingli himself. Grebel then looked upon Zwingli with eyes of love and admiration and hope, for it was inevitable, he thought, that Master Ulrich (*Huldrych* in Swiss) would cleanse and reform the Zurich church and restore it to New Testament purity.

At the time of the October 1523 Disputation (a theological debate on the issues facing the Zurich state church), Grebel became much disappointed with Zwingli's reformation program. Grebel wanted immediate action. Zwingli was minded to rely upon the Zurich council for the determination of the tempo of the reform. Why, asked Grebel, should the Mass not be abolished at once? And why does Zwingli not set up a free church of converted believers such as one finds in the New Testament? Grebel became impatient during the Disputation (October 26-28) and began to ask questions which reflected his earnest desire to obey the Scriptures: Since the Latin Bible calls the bread used in the communion *panis,* just why should not the church employ ordinary bread? And why should water be mixed into the communion wine when the New Testament gives no such instruction? Further, why should the officiating clergyman insert the wafer into the communicant's mouth as if he had no hands of his own? And if Christ instituted the communion service at night, perhaps that would be the time to observe it now! These questions were certainly not central in Grebel's mind, yet they do bear testimony to a seeking soul, hungering to align all of life with the written Word of God. Grebel's immediate concern, of course, remained the abolition of the Mass, for he saw no possibility of moving forward to the establishment of a truly New Testament church until the central papal ceremony was abolished. His deepest longing was to witness the creation of a free church of converted disciples such as one finds in the first-century Acts of the Apostles.

In an undated deposition of Zwingli, but stemming from late in 1525 or early in 1526, Zwingli testified that Simon Stumpf of Höngg (near Zurich), Conrad Grebel, and Felix Manz, had each come to him separately, "and more than once," requesting him to set up a separatist church which should live *aller unschuldigisten* (most piously). The consequence was, reported Zwingli, that they began to hold night meetings in the residence of the mother of Felix Manz. The meetings to which Zwingli alludes were the so-called "Bible schools," which were actually small Bible study groups.

The other issue which worried Grebel was the proper subjects of baptism. From Zwingli he had learned that it would be the part of wisdom to postpone baptism until the children of the church had come to years of understanding. Grebel was later to insist on this point, a rather galling reminder for Master Ulrich after he had firmly decided to retain infant baptism. (Zwingli was man enough to admit that this "error" had formerly misled him for a time.) Neither Zwingli nor Grebel assigned any supernatural efficacy to water baptism: for both it was a symbol. But for Grebel both the Christian life and church membership presupposed a free and personal commitment to Christ as Saviour and Lord. The baptism of infants would have made sense to Grebel if he could have brought himself to believe in baptismal regeneration. But Zwingli's teaching had so completely settled for him the symbolic character of baptism that he simply could not conceive of any form being scriptural except the baptism of accountable persons who had been converted through the gospel.

Zwingli, of course, continued with his glorious ministry of the Word in the Great Minster along the Limmat. Grebel began, as Zwingli reported, to hold Bible study classes in private homes in Zurich. He used the Greek New Testament, and expounded its rich truths to the small circle of friends who gathered around him. Likewise Felix Manz, illegitimate son of the Great Minster's chief canon, lectured to the group from the Hebrew Old Testament. They frequently met in the home of Manz's mother in Zurich.

Zwingli was finally goaded into action by Grebel and Manz and their supporters, who blamed him for being too mild in his reformation program. In December of 1524 he held a preliminary discussion with them, and on January 10, 1525, a second meeting took place. Finally, on Tuesday, January 17, 1525, a major disputation was held in Zurich before both the regular council and "the Great Council of the 200." Zwingli's opponents were Grebel, Manz, and Wilhelm Reublin, pastor of the church in Wytikon, near Zurich. All three "radicals" contended for the biblical basis of believer's baptism. But the councilmen were not convinced. On Wednesday, January 18, the Council announced that any parents who did not baptize their infants within eight days would be banished *mit wib, kind und sinem gut* (with wife, child, and property). On Saturday, January 21, the Zurich Council decreed that Grebel and Manz should cease holding their Bible classes and that they should stop "disputing." The following leaders were banished: Wilhelm Reublin (in Swiss, *Röubli*), pastor in Wytikon; Johannes Brötli, assistant pastor in Zollikon, a village near Zurich; Ludwig Haetzer, a Swiss priest and sympathizer with the Anabaptists; and Andreas Castelberger of Graubünden—none of them Zurich citizens.

Grebel and his friends now faced a crisis. They were officially forbidden to hold any more Bible study meetings. What should they do? They met together quietly that Saturday night, January 21, 1525, to think and pray and deliberate. An account of this meeting has been preserved in a sixteenth-century Anabaptist tome, *The Oldest Chronicle of the Hutterian Brethren,* the account probably having its source in a participant, George Blaurock. The group evidently came together to discuss how best to cope with the latest mandate of the Council. The *Chronicle* reports that "anxious fear" came upon them, and they were "moved in their hearts." Thereupon they knelt in prayer and called upon God to "enable them to do His divine will." An amazing scene then transpired. Following the prayer, George Blaurock, a former priest from the Swiss canton of Grisons, stepped up to Conrad Grebel, whom the group recognized as its natural leader, and asked for baptism. Blaurock knelt before Grebel and was baptized forthwith! The *Chronicle* rather naïvely explains that "at that time there was no ordained minister to perform such work." The others then asked George Blaurock to baptize them, which he did at once. Perhaps even more astonishing is the report: "Each ordained the other to the ministry of the Gospel." Thus the mandate which was intended to suppress forever the minority party which agitated for a free church, led instead to the actual establishment of the first free church! The die was cast, and Grebel either had to yield to what he felt was a mandate which violated his conscience, or defy the Zurich Council in the name of Christ. As a Christian he felt that he had no choice but to follow the Apostles of old and "obey God rather than men."

Grebel immediately plunged into a program of evangelism in the territory of Zurich. For ten days he stayed in his home community, but in February 1525, he removed to Schaffhausen where he remained as a missioner until toward the end of March when he returned to Zurich. Late in March and early in April he evangelized in St. Gall with great success. On Palm Sunday (April 9), 1525, he baptized large numbers of converts, so that the Anabaptist congregation there reached a reputed membership of 500. He returned to Zurich where he remained until June. Here he wrote his last letter which has been preserved; it was dated May 30, 1525, and addressed to his brother-in-law Vadian, reformer and civic leader in St. Gall, his "brother in the Lord." The letter is a vigorous plea not to attempt the suppression of Anabaptism by fines, confiscation of property, imprisonment, or death. Grebel solemnly declared that any blood shed in this matter is innocent blood: "Innocent it verily is, both if you know it and if you do not." The suffering of the Anabaptists, "and the end of their lives, and the great day of the Lord" will demonstrate their innocence.

But Anabaptist blood had been spilled already, although Grebel did not know it. On May 29, just the day before Grebel wrote, a minister of the Anabaptists named Eberli Bolt had been burned to death in his home town of Lachen in the Catholic canton of Schwyz. (He had been converted to the Anabaptist faith by some Anabaptists who escaped from prison in Zurich.) The Swiss chronicler Kessler reports that he went to the fire in good cheer, "and died willingly and undismayed."

The remaining months of Grebel's life rolled by rapidly.

About June 1525, he was in Waldshut briefly. Then for three months he evangelized in the Grüningen area east of Zurich, where he enjoyed the greatest success of his short preaching career. In July he was given a summons to stand trial in Zurich for "slandering" Zwingli's booklet on baptism. Upon being denied safe conduct he refused to present himself for trial. On October 8, however, he was apprehended at Hinwyl, whither he had gone to preach, and was imprisoned in the Grüningen castle. Meanwhile George Blaurock was arrested for his faith on October 8, 1525, and Manz was captured twenty-three days later. On November 6, Grebel and Manz were given a hearing by Zwingli; and twelve days later Grebel, Manz, and Blaurock were sentenced to prison on a diet of gruel, bread, and water, with no visitors permitted. There was a new trial on March 5-6, 1526, which eventuated in a sentence of life imprisonment. But strangely enough, the opportunity to escape came only two weeks later. After earnest debate (some of the imprisoned Anabaptists thought it not right to escape from a legally imposed sentence, while others regarded the rope which hung by their window as a divinely appointed means of escape) the group decided to flee. Grebel later turned up as a preacher and evangelist in Appenzell and *Graübunden,* or Grisons as it is called in English. In the village of Maienfeld in the canton of Grisons lived Grebel's oldest sister, and to her he evidently turned, hoping as a weary and sick man to find a bit of rest. But the plague struck him down, and he died in the summer of 1526, a young man of twenty-eight, broken in health and no doubt uncertain as to the very survival of his little group of followers.

The Spread of Anabaptism

Before many years had passed, the Anabaptists of Switzerland came to be known as Swiss Brethren. Congregations of the Swiss Brethren appeared not only in various cantons of German-speaking Switzerland, but in Alsace, Bavaria, Baden, Württemberg, Hesse, Thuringia, Franconia, the Palatinate, and the

Tirol. The two chief centers in South Germany for many years were Augsburg and Strasbourg, and the two most effective early leaders were Michael Sattler and Pilgram Marpeck. With the exception of Grebel, who died of the plague before the executioner was able to do away with him, most of the early leaders were executed for the "crime" of practicing the baptism of adults, and for setting up free churches, that is, congregations which were not a part of a state or territorial church. State churches were established by civil law as the required religion of the territory. (The state or territorial churches were Catholic, Lutheran, or Reformed, depending upon the territory involved.)

The First Martyr in Zurich

One of the most attractive figures in early Swiss Anabaptism was Felix Manz. Manz was born about the year 1498, the son of a Zurich canon. A master of Hebrew, Greek, and Latin, Manz put all his talents to work in the building up of the Anabaptist Brotherhood through evangelism and nurture. Late in March 1525, Manz was imprisoned along with thirteen men and seven women of the Anabaptist group in the building known as the *Hexenturm* (witch tower) in Zurich. These twenty-one religious prisoners managed to make their escape on April 5, perhaps with the connivance of friends and sympathizers. Within two weeks Manz had resumed baptizing converts. But he was soon captured and was given a thorough examination. He stated openly that he had never rejected the institution of human government, nor had he opposed the charging of interest, nor the payment of the compulsory tithes of that period in Switzerland. He admitted being opposed to capital punishment and to "the sword," that is, to participation in warfare. He had not taught "community of goods," which meant a congregation having "all things common," following the primitive Christians at Jerusalem (Acts 4:32). Manz stated that he had taught only that Christians should be willing to share with those who were in need. The Zurich authorities were sufficiently satisfied to release him.

Following his release Manz evangelized briefly in Grüningen in the canton of Zurich. By the middle of May he was at Chur in the canton of Grisons, working co-operatively with George Blaurock. On July 18 he was apprehended by the authorities and returned to Zurich for imprisonment. The magistrate at Chur reported that Manz could not be dissuaded from preaching and baptizing people, even by the threat of death. "He is an obstinate and recalcitrant person." Manz was imprisoned in the Wellenberg prison in Zurich until October 7, 1525. He was then freed, only to be arrested on October 30 for renewed activity as an Anabaptist. He was in and out of prison a number of times during the winter of 1525-26. On March 7, 1526, he was imprisoned for life. But in a month or so he had somehow regained his freedom. In April he was evangelizing in Grisons and Appenzell. He was once more captured December 3, 1526, for his final imprisonment. On January 5, 1527, the Zurich authorities sentenced him to death by drowning—a mode designed to show in what great dishonor he was to be executed, for execution by drowning was the customary mode for women. The sentence included the following details:

> Manz shall be delivered to the executioner, who shall tie his hands, put him into a boat, take him to the lower hut [in the Limmat river which flows through the city of Zurich], there strip his bound hands down over his knees, place a stick between his knees and arms [locking him in a doubled-up position], and thus push him into the water, and let him perish.[3]

As Manz was being bound he sang out in Latin, *In manus tuas, Domine, commendo spiritum meum* (Into thy hands, O Lord, I commend my spirit). Thus perished the first Anabaptist martyr in Reformed territory.

George Blaurock, Evangelist

The first man baptized by Conrad Grebel on January 21, 1525, was a former priest named George of the House of Jacob. He soon became a dynamic evangelist, with perhaps a touch of

what would now be considered fanaticism; at least he is reported on one occasion to have taken over a Reformed minister's
pulpit without permission. He was born in Bonaduz, a village
in Grisons, Switzerland, and served as a Roman priest prior
to his conversion to Anabaptism. He is described as a tall
man with a powerful physique, fiery eyes, black hair, and a
small bald spot. His real name was George of the House of Jacob,
but his common appellation stemmed from his habit of wearing a blue coat (*Blaurock* in German). A man of tremendous
energy, he went about Switzerland as an evangelist, warning
sinners to turn to Christ and to seal their faith with water
baptism. Many converts accepted his message and united with the
Swiss Brethren. On the day of Manz's execution, Blaurock as a
noncitizen of Zurich was stripped to the waist and beaten with
rods as he was marched from the Fish Market to the Niederdorf
gate and expelled from the city. His last field of evangelism
was the Tirol: Clausen, Guffidaun, Ritten, Vels, and Breitenberg.
Here he gathered the scattered Anabaptists and strengthened
their faith. On June 2, 1529, a Tirolese Anabaptist preacher
and pastor named Michael Kürschner was burned at the stake
by the Catholic authorities, and Blaurock hastened to take
charge of the pastorless flock. The Tirolese authorities sought
to apprehend him, and on August 14, 1529, they were able to
report success. On August 24 he was severely tortured, and on
September 6 burned at the stake. He was executed on a fivefold
charge: (1) he left the priesthood, (2) taught against infant
baptism, (3) repudiated the Mass, (4) rejected the confessional,
and (5) taught that people should not pray to Mary the mother
of Christ. It has been estimated that he won a thousand
converts in the short period of his evangelistic career.

Michael Sattler and the Seven Articles

One of the most attractive figures of the Swiss Brethren movement was Michael Sattler of Staufen in Breisgau, South Germany.
He came to Zurich soon after the establishment of Anabaptism

and united with the Brethren there. Banished from Zurich on November 18, 1525, he removed to southern Württemberg and became an active evangelist in that territory. On February 24, 1527, he presided at an Anabaptist meeting at Schleitheim, a Swiss village near Schaffhausen, and the Anabaptists present adopted a confession of faith which he had written, entitled *Brotherly Union of a Number of Children of God Concerning Seven Articles*. These seven articles treat of: (1) Baptism. This sign shall be performed on those who have turned from sin and are living a holy Christian life, who believe that Christ has taken away their sins, who wish to die with Christ and to "walk in the resurrection of Jesus Christ," and who request it for themselves. This excludes infant baptism, "the chief abomination of the pope." (2) Excommunication (the "ban"). A brother or sister in the church who lapses into sin shall twice be warned in secret, and the third time openly excommunicated according to the word of Christ in Matthew 18. Any disciplinary cases in the church shall be taken care of before the communion of the Lord's Supper so that a united church may eat and drink in love. (3) The Breaking of Bread. Christians must be united beforehand, by baptism, in the one Body of which Christ is the Head, if they wish to commune together. Members of Christ's church cannot commune with those who are not walking in the obedience of Christ. (4) Separation from the World. God calls upon his children to come out of the world and to have no fellowship with those who are not in Christ. This separation involves breaking spiritual and social fellowship with papal and Reformed church services alike (all churches were then calling for the death penalty for Anabaptists), no patronizing of drinking houses, and no participation in civic matters, that is, no participation in the magistracy. (5) Pastors in the Church. The pastor or shepherd (*Hirt*) is to be a man with a good name. He shall read God's Word to the people, admonish and teach them, warn and discipline, excommunicate, lift up the bread in the communion service, and lead out in the prayers of the church. He shall receive his support from the gifts of the church (not from taxes or beneficences). If a given pastor is martyred, another shall be chosen at once so that the church may not be destroyed. (6) Nonresistance. Outside the church God has ordained the sword for the maintenance of law and order in a wicked society. The sword of Moses passed to the magistrates of the world (not to the church). The only way the church can deal with wicked sinners is to excommunicate them. Members of the church must follow under all circumstances the law of love and the example of Christ in his non-resistant suffering. (7) The Oath. Because of the express prohibition of Christ, Christians ought not to swear under any circumstances. Swearing is not consistent with the finite limitations of earthly creatures. God can swear because in his omnipotence he has no limitations and can perfectly carry out his intentions. (Even today Mennonites still baptize after personal conversion and commitment, and upon confession of faith; they practice church discipline, excommunicating those who cease to live a holy life; they generally practice "close communion"; they maintain an emphasis on "nonconformity to the world"; they insist on high standards of life on the part of their ministers, and many congregations still give their pastors "love offerings" rather than a stipulated salary; they hold strictly to nonresistance, and therefore refuse to serve in the military; and they give only a solemn affirmation of the truth in lieu of the legal oath.)

Zwingli considered Sattler's Schleitheim Articles of Faith to possess sufficient merit to write a refutation of them in Part Two of his *Elenchus* (1527). And John Calvin based his polemic against the Anabaptists in part upon the Schleitheim Articles: *A Brief Instruction to Equip All the Good Saints Against the Errors of the Communistic Sect of the Anabaptists*, 1544.

It was but a short time after the Schleitheim meeting until Sattler "of the white overcoat," as he is called in the Zurich archives, was arrested and tried as a heretic. He was arrested at Horb in Württemberg, imprisoned in Binsdorf (whence he wrote a moving letter to the Anabaptist congregation at Horb, urging them to faithful adherence to their confession, and to a faithful Christian life), and tried at Rottenburg on the Neckar, a city in Catholic Austrian territory. The trial took place May 17-18, 1527. Nine charges were brought against Sattler: (1) He was guilty of disobedience to the imperial mandates, all of which had, from the Diet of Worms in 1521, sanctioned only one faith within the Holy Roman Empire, that of the Roman Catholic Church (Sattler denied disobedience, for he claimed that the mandates called only for adherence to the Word of God). (2) He denied the real presence of Christ in the sacrament (this charge he admitted). (3) He taught that infant baptism does not conduce to salvation (this he admitted teaching). (4) He rejected the sacrament of extreme unction (he claimed not to reject the oil of James 5, but denied that said oil was "the pope's oil"). (5) He despised and condemned the Mother of God and the saints (he denied the charge, but held that Mary was not a Mediatress; the saints are simply the believers, and "the blessed" are those who have died). (6) He taught that men should not swear before the authorities (this he admitted, basing his position on the word of Christ). (7) He inaugurated a new form of the Lord's Supper, eating the bread and wine from a plate (he made no recorded reply, but this he evidently learned from Zwingli, for that is how the Lord's Supper was set up in Zurich in Holy Week, 1525). (8) He had abandoned his Catholic order and married a wife (he claimed that this was his right, for the New Testament condemns compulsory celibacy). (9) He taught that Christians ought not to fight against the Turks, and that if he had his choice he would rather fight on the side of the Turks, if war were right (he replied that Christians ought not indeed to take life, but should cry to God for his protection; the reason for his remark about siding with the Turks was that they knew no better, while the professing Christians who killed the Turks were "Turks after the spirit").

After this he suffered some abuse in court—the clerk declared that if there were no other executioner, he himself would destroy Sattler and reckon that he had done God a service! When Sattler attempted to reason with him, the clerk cut him off, saying that the hangman would dispute with him, "You arch heretic!" After retiring, the judges re-entered the room and passed sentence that Sattler should be led to the place of execution, his tongue should be cut off, his body should six times be torn with red-hot tongs, and then he should be burned to powder as a heretic. The date of his death was May 21, 1527. His wife was executed by drowning a few days later. A description of Sattler's trial and death was written to the the Swiss Anabaptists in the Zurich area by Wilhelm Reublin. The account of his martyrdom, together with his letter to the Horb congregation, was soon printed in booklet form, and both found a place in the *Martyrs Mirror*, 1660.

Pilgram Marpeck

One of the most interesting leaders of the South German and Swiss Anabaptists was a man named Pilgram Marpeck. A native of the Tirol, his home was at Rattenberg on the Inn River. By 1520 he was married, and in that year he was received into the miners' brotherhood of Rattenberg. By 1523 he was a member of the outer council of the city and by 1525 of the inner council. In the latter year he was appointed a mining judge with an annual salary of sixty-five pounds, with an additional three pounds allowed for court dress. That he was a young man of wealth is evident from the fact that in 1525 he loaned 1,000 guilders to the state treasury. (A guilder or florin in Austria was roughly the equivalent of an American dollar.) He also owned at least two houses. Just when Marpeck turned to Anabaptism is not known. The movement had reached Rattenberg by 1527, and on January 28 of the next year Marpeck was removed from his office. Two weeks before this an Anabaptist leader named Leonard Schiemer was executed as a martyr in Rattenberg; and on February 4 another, named Hans Schlaffer, met the same fate. Marpeck found it advisable to flee Rattenberg. His property was confiscated at once. In 1529, when he should have received his inheritance, in value perhaps 3,500 guilders, that too was confiscated.

About February 1528, Marpeck, with his wife Anna, left Rattenberg. But where should he go? With all security gone Marpeck became a sort of pilgrim on the face of the earth. It is reported that he first located in Augsburg. In October 1528 he arrived in Strasbourg, where he soon became the leader of the Anabaptist congregation. He did not live in the city at first; his residence was in a nearby village, Steintal. Soon he was employed in the city forest some twenty-five miles southwest of Strasbourg. He had been known in Rattenberg as a man with engineering gifts, and he now put his talent to work for the city of Strasbourg. He constructed a complex system of waterways and wood-floating flumes in the valleys of the Ehn and Brerisch in Alsace, and of the Kinzig and Murg in Baden. When he moved to the city of Strasbourg in 1530 he was at first a popular man; his followers, it was said, honored him like a god. Even the state clergy were fond of him for a time. But he was an outspoken man and given to sharp language. He not only taught the principle of believer's baptism, but he labeled infant baptism a "sacrifice to Moloch," words which understandably did not increase the love of the state clergy for him. Martin Bucer, a leading theologian in Strasbourg, regarded him as self-willed, although Bucer admitted that Marpeck and wife were both of unblamable character. By the year 1531 Marpeck felt constrained to call for a public debate with the clergy. A colloquium was granted him on December 9 of that year, but not a public one; the discussion was held before the city council and the so-called Committee of Twenty-one. (Sometime before this Marpeck was imprisoned briefly, but the intercession of a prominent churchman of Strasbourg, Wolfgang Capito, and probably Marpeck's own valuable work with the waterways, effected his release. He had written two booklets defending the doctrine of nonresistance and opposing the swearing of oaths, but the city censors had suppressed them.) The outcome of the colloquium was that Marpeck was ordered to leave if he stuck to his erroneous views that infant baptism ought to be discarded and if he intended to set up a separatist church. He in turn requested a period of grace to allow him opportunity to sell his home. He also managed to have another disputation on January 18, 1532, but again he failed to convince the council of the biblical basis for his position. So once more he took to the road. The old records indicate that he was back in Strasbourg in 1534, but only briefly. In 1540 he wrote a letter from near Ilanz in Grisons. The next year he seems to have visited the Hutterian Brethren in Moravia. In 1544 he was again in Grisons. That same year he located in Augsburg, and here he managed to live until his death in 1556. During his residence in Augsburg he secured employment with the city, and he is referred to in the city records as the *Stadtwerckmeister,* probably a sort of city engineer. All the while, of course, he was also busy as an Anabaptist leader. The consequence was that the civil authorities were annoyed; they sent him warnings about his Anabaptist activities in 1545, 1550, 1553, and 1554, but he was not to be intimidated.

Marpeck is remembered for two reasons: for his long and tedious controversy with the Spiritualist, Caspar Schwenckfeld von Ossig, who claimed that the Anabaptists had no right to set up a church organization; and for his literary efforts.

In 1542 Marpeck translated and revised a new edition of Bernt Rothmann's book of 1533, *Confession of Both Sacraments, Baptism and Lord's Supper.* The book, however, gives no indication either of the original writer nor of its translator and reviser. Schwenckfeld at once wrote a *Judicium* (critique) of the volume, attacking it at many points. This unprovoked attack was a source of irritation to Marpeck, and he and his colleagues wrote an enormous manuscript *Answer* to Schwenckfeld, which was published for the first time in 1929. In the course of preparing the *Answer* it became clear to Marpeck that what was really needed was a treatise setting forth the contrast between the Old and New Covenants. This was accordingly prepared and printed, the *Testament Explanation.* The period of the Old Testament, "Yesterday," was set over against "Today" on a vast array of subjects: grace, forgiveness, salvation, sword, and many others. The thesis of the book is that the period prior to Christ's incarnation was one of promise, while this age is that of fulfillment. There was no real forgiveness prior to Calvary, for Christ's sacrifice had not yet been offered.

Recent research suggests that Marpeck's Anabaptist followers may not have been one group with the Swiss Brethren, although any differences were trivial. Indeed he labored long and hard to effect one large and united brotherhood of all the Anabaptists, which union seems to have been accomplished at a conference in Strasbourg in 1555. Marpeck was one of the few Anabaptist leaders prior to 1530 who did not die a martyr's death.

Anabaptist Tracts

Larger books such as the *Answer* to Schwenckfeld and the *Testament Explanation* were but rarely written by Swiss and South German Anabaptists. Their literary efforts were for the most part confined to tracts. One of the most effective of these tracts was a little jewel entitled *Two Kinds of Obedience,* which appeared in the period 1525-30. The anonymous writer, perhaps Sattler himself, begins by explaining that the two kinds of obedience are filial, which springs from love for God, and servile, which is selfish in character. Filial obedience, that of a child, is far better and more effective than the servile variety, that of a slave. Only Christian freedom makes possible the creation of Christian character. Legalism, whether of the Old Testament type or a more modern vintage, starves the souls of men. Law had, to be sure, a good function; it was to prepare sinners for redemption. Apart from the law of God men would go to perdition, drowned in an ocean of "love for the creature." The author makes quite a point of the higher ethical standards of the New Testament—the theological justification which the Anabaptists commonly made for such doctrines as nonresistance and the rejection of the civil oath. This tract dispels once and for all the notion that the Anabaptists held to a weak view of grace,

or that they believed in "works-righteousness." It demonstrates
that the Anabaptists had a keen awareness of the grace of God, a
wholesome emphasis on love, and a fear of every kind of legalism.
The tract closes with a ringing reminder that the church will
not always be a maligned and persecuted body; the day will
come when the tabernacle of God will be among men, and he
shall dwell with them and be their God, and they shall be his
people.

Another interesting tract from the same period is *Concerning
the Satisfaction of Christ*. Writers as early as the Dutch martyrologist, P. J. Twisck (1565-1636), ascribed it to Michael Sattler,
with good grounds but no absolute proof. One picks up this
tract expecting it to be a brief treatise on the atonement of
Christ, but it turns out to be a discussion of the question, "To
whom do the blessings of the atonement apply?" Who is it that can
make the claim, "Christ died for me"? The writer holds that the
atonement is potentially universal in its scope. Although it would
be sufficient for all men, if they became believers on Christ, yet
it is actually efficacious only for those who really believe. And
who are the believers? What does it mean to have faith? Far
more, insists the writer, than renouncing Catholicism, the religion of works. And far more than making the ("Protestant")
claim that Christ is our mercy seat. It is not a mere matter of
lip profession. To have faith is to live the Christian life, to follow
Christ in holiness, love, and obedience. Real faith is not a matter
of works of merit, but it does involve being prepared to take up
the cross and follow Jesus Christ even to the martyr's stake. And
only those who take up the cross and follow Christ have the
right to think of themselves as Christians. So what starts out
to be a treatise on the atonement ends up as a call to what we
would now call existential Christianity. Yet with all his emphasis
on good works and obedience, the author avoids the pitfall of
human merit. He recognizes that a good Christian life is not a
matter of human volition but is the fruit of God's working
within. The writer closes on a rather bitter note as he laments
that the Reformers stopped short in their program by their re-

tention of infant baptism. He regards this as nothing less awful than the second beast of Revelation 13—the beast which calls down fire from heaven upon its opponents (a protest against the violent suppression of Anabaptism). Little wonder that the tract closes with the New Testament call: "Come out of her, my people . . ."

Another fine example of 'Anabaptist theology is the little tract entitled *Concerning Divorce,* also of the first years of the Anabaptist movement. P. J. Twisck (1565-1636), who was married to Menno Simons' granddaughter, assigned it to Sattler. The anonymous author begins by asserting that monogamous marriage was God's original plan for the race, but that Moses permitted divorce for rather trivial reasons. It was Jesus who restored the original *Ordnung* (regulation or ordinance) of God; and he permitted divorce for only one reason: marital infidelity. Christ's word on this subject is only one example of his advance over the lower ethical standards of the Old Testament. But, says the tract, if one is married to an unbeliever, it is likely that the Christian life and witness of the believer will so arouse the enmity of the non-Christian as to terminate the union. In any case the Christian's union with Christ is more significant than any earthly marriage. It is better to separate from an unbelieving spouse than to suffer damage to one's spiritual life. The main thrust of the tract is not on divorce and its limitation at all; rather it is on the primacy of loyalty to Christ. Nevertheless, the church must scrupulously obey her Lord; she cannot therefore tolerate remarriage unless the divorce was granted because of unfaithfulness to the marriage vows.

Mention must also be made of the vigorous Anabaptist polemic of Martin Weninger, nicknamed Lingki, entitled *Rechenschaft (Vindication),* 1535. Little is known of Lingki's life. He was banished from Zurich in November 1525, the same day as Michael Sattler. Six years later an Anabaptist named Flückiger reported that he had been baptized the previous Easter by a leader named Lingki. Lingki also served as the chief spokesman for the Swiss Brethren in the disputation or debate held between

the Anabaptists and the Reformed at Zofingen, Canton Berne, in
1532. Haller, the Reformed leader of Berne, described Lingki
as "a learned and cunning man, an eloquent and amazing hypo-
crite, especially gifted in deception"—which is another illustra-
tion of sixteenth-century polemics. When Lingki, in the course
of the Zofingen debate, demanded scriptural proof for infant
baptism, the Reformed spokesman replied, "Dear Lingki, tell
me where it is written that the apostles baptized a German or
a Swabian."

Weninger's *Vindication* may be said to provide the standard
Swiss Brethren statement as to why they withdrew from the state
church. Fully aware of their own depravity, the Brethren nevertheless felt that unless a professing believer lived a holy life he
was not one of Christ's disciples. The evident carnality of many
state churchmen, even of numbers of the clergy, compelled grave
doubts about their salvation and about the right of their fellowship to be considered a true church. Some of Weninger's statements, taken alone, could actually be interpreted as teaching a
naïve perfectionism; yet in the Zofingen disputation he said ex-
pressly: "In me there is nothing good. I am unable of myself
even to think anything that is good, but am as others flesh and
blood, and subject to temptation. But that I should let these
reign I answer, No. Therefore God must give me grace to overcome." Weninger was one of the few Anabaptists who returned
to the Reformed Church. It is not known what considerations
of logic or torture or threatened martyrdom moved him to publicly renounce Anabaptism at Schaffhausen in 1538.

The *Vindication* was bitterly critical of the "hirelings," the
salaried clergy of the state church, whom Lingki regarded as
bloodthirsty (because of the executions of Swiss Brethren leaders
which they incited). Furthermore, these state church clergy
"teach contrary to Paul (Romans 6) that one cannot be free of
sin and live in righteousness: 'One must sin to the grave; no one
can keep the commandments of God' (I John 3, 5), which is not
true." Thereupon he quotes all sorts of passages on the victory
over sin which Christ has enabled his saints to attain by his

atoning death. But Lingki asserted that when he inspected the lives of the members of the state church he found all sorts of gross sin tolerated: "adulterers, heavy drinkers, blasphemers, misers, usurers, dancers . . . without a ban to make any difference." This absence of church discipline was, in the mind of Lingki, simply fatal. Of course, he continued, the priests who ought to discipline such open sinners are unable to do so for the simple reason that they themselves live the same way! But the true children of God are those who allow him to work out his gracious will in their lives, and such holy people are acceptable to him. As Lingki put it in his Swiss German—and these are the closing words of the tract—*Der recht thut uss forcht Gottes ist Gott angenäm* (The right done from the fear of God is acceptable to him).

Swiss Anabaptism and Other Movements

Modern research has revealed that besides the three main streams of the Reformation, that is, Lutheran, Reformed, and Anglican, there were three similar Anabaptist movements: (1) the original Swiss Anabaptists, or Swiss Brethren, founded by Conrad Grebel; (2) the Austrian branch of the movement which added the Christian "community of goods" (compare Acts 4:34-35) to its practice, the so-called Hutterian Brethren, named for Jacob Hutter who was burned at the stake February 25, 1536, at Innsbruck in the Austrian Tirol; (3) the Dutch Anabaptists, later known as Mennists (now Mennonites) after Menno Simons; as well as (4) the free-lance movement led by an independent ex-Lutheran named Melchior Hofmann, which—contrary to Hofmann's intentions—culminated in the awful Münster episode in Westphalia, 1534-35. (The Spiritualists and the anti-Trinitarians constituted additional and basically independent streams, as Professor Fritz Blanke of Zürich has pointed out.[4]) The first three Anabaptist groups were never totally destroyed, and today number several hundred thousand in Europe and the Americas, the Mennonites, while the Münsterite movement with all its

tragedy and horror lasted for only a few short years in the sixteenth century. But the memory of Münster served for four centuries to obscure and divert attention from the true nature of
original Anabaptism with its remarkable concept of Christian
discipleship.

II

ANABAPTISTS
IN THE NETHERLANDS

✠

Melchior Hofmann

One of the most enigmatical reformers of the sixteenth century was an ex-Lutheran preacher and free-lance Anabaptist named Melchior Hofmann. Born about 1495 in Swabian Hall, Melchior was by profession a furrier. Devout, able, sincere, and possessing a rare knowledge of the Bible, he was able to move the masses to repentance and faith. He wrote voluminously. A man of tremendous energy, he preached betimes at Strasbourg, Stockholm, Emden, Amsterdam. Everywhere he stirred up considerable excitement and commotion. Luther was at first kindly disposed toward him, but eventually became cool and critical, holding that Hofmann ought to return to his furrier's trade, for he was not competent to preach, nor was he called. Hofmann did not formally unite with any Anabaptist group until 1530. To the end he was critical of the Swiss Brethren, and they of him. In the disputation of 1538, held in Bern, Switzerland, the Brethren reported that he was not named a brother among them, and that they had resisted his teaching "with all earnestness."

Hofmann agreed with the Swiss Anabaptists on a number of points. He believed in freedom of conscience, in holiness of life, in believer's baptism, and in nonresistance. In his earlier period he rejected the oath unconditionally, but later gave it limited approval. His greatest difference with the Swiss Brethren, however, was in two fields: (1) he was overwhelmed by apocalypticism, and wrote one booklet after another dealing with end-time events on which he thought his understanding was as clear as crystal, and which he announced were to break upon the world no later than 1534; (2) he conceived a strange theory to account for the human nature of Christ as well as his sinlessness: Mary, declared Melchior, gave birth to the Lord Jesus, and yet he did not partake of her nature. Christ was the Lord from heaven who was conceived of the Holy Ghost. Christ's body was in Mary but not of Mary. (This view later caused much difficulty in Dutch Anabaptism until its abandonment.) The final cleavage with the Swiss Brethren came when Hofmann decided to defer baptism of his converts for a couple of years, as well as to wait for the actual creation of a separatist church until a more propitious era. For the Swiss Anabaptists this program was plain cowardice, even sinful disobedience to the Lord Jesus, for it was he who had issued the Great Commission. The followers of Hofmann in the Netherlands—"Melchiorites" or *Bontgenooten* (comrades in the covenant) they were called—actually remained a small and secret party within the Roman Church, awaiting the day when Hofmann would be divinely led to move ahead with the establishment of a church.

The significance of Hofmann for Dutch Anabaptism lies in this fact: It was he who baptized one Jan Matthijs of Haarlem, and Jan in turn broke with Hofmann on his waiting two years to inaugurate baptism. Late in 1533 Jan sent out twelve "apostles" to preach and to baptize. Two of them, Bartel Boeckbinder and Willem Cuper, went to Leeuwarden in Friesland and baptized Obbe Philips in December 1533, and the next day ordained him as an elder. Obbe in turn baptized a converted priest named Menno Simons a little over two years later (1536), and Menno became the eponymous leader of the Dutch Mennists (or present-day Mennonites).

Hofmann's fanaticism meanwhile went from bad to worse. A visionary Anabaptist of the same stripe as he, a man of Friesland, prophesied that Hofmann would return to Strasbourg, be arrested, and lie in jail half a year, whereupon the Lord's Second Coming would take place. At that point, declared the Frisian seer, Hofmann would lead forth an Anabaptist procession over all the world! This was marvelous news, and in an expectant mood Hofmann hurried back to Strasbourg. When his imprisonment had not taken place after two months he himself solicited arrest. The council obliged him with a prompt imprisonment in May 1533. The poor deluded "Elijah" lay in jail for ten years, much of the time in a miserable state with no visitors permitted, and denied the use of paper, pen, and ink, and with his food supplied through a hole in the ceiling. He filled anything that would receive impressions with a record of his odd ideas, and some of the writings, recorded on twenty-four pieces of cloth, were preserved as archival material in Strasbourg until destroyed by fire in 1870. Death finally came to the poor man, honest but misguided soul that he was, in 1543. Christ had not come, and there were no 144,000 adherents of the truth ready to greet him. Hofmann believed that only he and his supporters had the truth. "Alas, what a terrible time is this," he wrote in 1531, "that I do not yet see a true evangelist, nor know any writer among all the German people who witnesses to the true faith and the everlasting Gospel."

The Kingdom of Münster

The full tragedy of a degenerate "Melchiorism" was ushered in by Jan Matthijs of Haarlem, one of whose "apostles" baptized Obbe Philips. Jan was a deluded fanatic of the first water. As early as 1531 Münster in Westphalia was being influenced by a former priest named Bernt Rothmann who was now preaching Lutheran doctrine, and who had been both to Wittenberg and Strasbourg. In 1532 the Reformation in Münster grew by leaps and bounds, so that by August evangelical preachers occupied all the pulpits of the city except the cathedral. Gradually the reform movement of the city was divided into two wings, a conservative Lutheran group and a more radical wing which proved to be susceptible to the most fanatical and wild ideas. Münster had in it some peaceful Melchiorites, and by January 1534, some of the "apostles" of the foolish Jan Matthijs had arrived as well.

As Dr. Christian Neff wrote in his article on the Münster Anabaptists in the *Mennonitisches Lexikon,* "Gradually peaceful Anabaptism grew into a caricature." An opportunist named Knipperdolling became mayor of the city in February 1534, a few weeks after the radicals of the city had seized the city hall. Four days after Knipperdolling got control, believer's baptism was made compulsory; all who refused it were to get out of the city forthwith. Hofmann's wild apocalypticism, although peaceful in character in his own mind, had so confused the masses as to destroy their ability to recognize even a mad delusion. The consequence was that many severely persecuted Anabaptists fled toward Münster, believing that there, rather than Strasbourg, was to be the capital of the Lord's heavenly Kingdom. Jan Matthijs tried to achieve a glorious victory, like an Old Testament military hero, and was promptly slain by the Catholic bishop's army which had laid siege to the city. The man who exploited the situation in his own favor was a former innkeeper named Jan Beuckelsz of Leiden, certainly the worst of the twelve "apostles" of Jan Matthijs. Beuckelsz had come to Münster in January 1534, and by the summer of that year he had gained control of the government and was reigning as an absolute despot. In July he introduced polygamy, after executing those who withstood his plan. In September he took the title of king. With his harem he lived in ease and splendor, and he displayed genuine cunning in maintaining the morale of the city in spite of hunger. He was able to keep the bishop's army at bay until the night of June 24-25, 1535. The capture of the city brought a sudden end to King Jan's glory, and deliverance came to his starving subjects. The "king" was executed a year and a half later, along with two of his henchmen, and their corpses were hung in iron cages on the tower of St. Lambert Church. The cages are still there. The damage done by the ultra-Melchiorism in the sick minds of the two Jans also remains unto this day, for the caricature of the Reformation which is known as the kingdom of Münster is in the minds of many people a sample of the meaning of Anabaptism. This is equivalent to pinning the blame for the Peasants' Revolt in Germany onto the great reformer of Wittenberg in Saxony!

The Philips Brothers

Obbe and Dirk Philips were the illegitimate sons of a Dutch priest. As was mentioned before, Obbe was baptized in December 1533 by two of Jan Matthijs's "apostles," Bartel Boeckbinder and Willem Cuper (or Cuiper). Dirk Philips, a Franciscan monk prior to his conversion, was baptized by Pieter Houtzagher, another "apostle," a week later, near the close of 1533. Both baptisms occurred at Leeuwarden in Friesland where the Philips brothers lived. The Matthijs "apostles" assembled about fifteen prospective converts at Leeuwarden, including Obbe Philips, and reported on the miracle-working power of Matthijs. Obbe was overwhelmed by the account, naïvely unaware of how deceptive false prophets could be. Best of all was the promise of the "apostles" that no blood would be shed in persecution, because God was about to clear the earth of all the godless tyrants and persecutors. Obbe had some inner anxiety as to whether this promise was really true, but like the others he was afraid to speak his mind in opposition to the "commissioned" emissaries of Matthijs. The three Matthijs "apostles" who had baptized the Philips brothers believed their own testimony that they were immune to persecution, and in March 1534 they marched through Amsterdam crying out that the "new city" (the west side of Amsterdam where the Melchiorites gathered) was blessed, while the "old city" was cursed: "Woe, woe, to all the godless!" The proclaimers of woe were promptly arrested and were shortly "tortured to death" at Haarlem, along with about fifteen other Melchiorites. Obbe went to the place of execution and inspected the heap of severed heads and smoked and broken bodies to ascertain which were the three who had baptized himself and his brother Dirk. But the torture on the wheel, as well as the fire and smoke, had so changed the appearance of the dead as to make identification impossible.

It was probably early in 1534 that Obbe ordained his own brother Dirk to the office of bishop ("elder") in the Dutch Anabaptist brotherhood. Great confusion then obtained among the Anabaptists of the Low Countries. Who was right, Melchior Hofmann with his mild message of repentance, nonresistance, and holiness? Or the revolutionary fanatics who thought that God wanted the saints to take the sword against the godless, the movement which came to full fruition at Münster? Obbe and Dirk resisted the revolutionary tendencies. The execution of the men who had baptized them, and who had ordained Obbe as elder, also served to disillusion the Philips brothers. Their eyes were opened to the unreliable character of the apocalypticism preached by the Melchiorite "apostles." Obbe and Dirk took up in 1534 the task of shepherding the peaceful wing of the Melchiorites. Three years later, early in 1537, Obbe ordained the converted Roman priest, Menno Simons of Witmarsum in Friesland, to the office of "Obbenite" elder, the service taking place in the Dutch province of Groningen.

At an early date a marked difference in program between Obbe on the one hand, and Menno and Dirk on the other, became painfully apparent. Obbe's emphasis fell increasingly on a sort of individualistic piety in which each man was to concentrate on attaining for himself a vital spiritual life of deep communion with God. Menno and Dirk, however, were congregation-centered in their thinking; they were determined to set up a fellowship of truly converted people, each group to be a well-disciplined unit of love and fellowship, obedient to Christ and his Word, especially to the New Testament. Which emphasis was to triumph—Obbe, or Dirk and Menno? It turned out that it was the strict congregationalism of Dirk and Menno, in contrast with the individualism of Obbe, which was destined to be victorious. The consequence was that Obbe abandoned the movement by 1540, sick at heart over his questionable commission by such fanatics as the "apostles" of Matthijs. But Menno and Dirk moved vigorously forward and established a chain of congregations in the Netherlands and North Germany, each exercising a strict biblical discipline over the members. Dirk finally settled in Danzig, although he traveled about much, as he sought to build up the congregations against all the obstacles which they faced: persecutions from without and problems of unity within, problems often associated with how strictly to apply the ban and *shunning*. (Strange as it may seem, Obbe had inaugurated shunning or avoidance—the breaking of all social fellowship with excommunicated persons—to keep his followers safe from the revolutionary and fanatical Münsterites. A few small bodies of American Mennonites, especially the so-called Old Order Amish, still *shun* excommunicated members.)

Both Obbe and Dirk Philips left writings for their followers. About the year 1560 Obbe, a rather weary and bitter old man, wrote his booklet, *A Confession,* which has recently been published in English.[1] Dirk died in 1568, leaving behind a number of books and booklets which were published as a single volume in five Dutch editions from 1564 to 1627; seven German editions, 1715 to 1917; and one English edition, 1910, entitled, *Enchiridion or Hand Book of the Christian Doctrine and Religion.*[2]

Menno Simons, Christocentric Churchman

About the year 1496 there was born to a Dutchman named Simon a son whom he named Menno. In accord with the custom of the time and place the child was called Menno Simonsz (for Simon's son), or simply Simons. As a young man Menno prepared for the Roman priesthood, and in 1524 he was consecrated as priest. As a student he learned Latin, church history, patristics, and the like, but no Bible. Indeed, he had never read in the Bible at all by the time he began in his first parish, Pingjum, in 1524. Up to this point Menno was a convinced Catholic with no notion that he would ever turn to an evangelical faith. Three incidents drove him to change his mind. (1) During the first year of his priesthood, while engaged in the celebration of the Mass, the thought suddenly struck him that perhaps the doctrine of transubstantiation was after all not true. Menno was shocked

at this attack from the devil—for so he interpreted the idea—
and he sought to dismiss it from his mind. It turned out that he
was unable to do so. He went to the confessional. He sought help
from his superiors. But all in vain. The idea would not down.
In desperation he took up the New Testament and was amazed
to learn that it did not seem to uphold the Roman view of the
sacrament. He also turned to Luther's writings and by 1528 was
fully convinced by the Wittenberg reformer that the rejection of
a human doctrine could not lead to eternal death. (2) In 1531
a second incident disturbed Menno; he heard of the execution of a
man named Sicke Freerks Snijder for being rebaptized. Never
in all his life had Menno heard of anything like a second baptism. He began to wonder whether the Catholic Church might
have an unbiblical view of baptism as well as of the sacrament
of communion. He could find nothing to satisfy him on the
question of why infants should be baptized, either in the New
Testament or in the writings of the Protestant Reformers. Still
Menno continued as a Roman priest, baptizing babies, hearing
confessions, and celebrating the Mass. (3) In 1535 his own brother
was swept along in the Dutch whirlpool of revolutionary Anabaptism and lost his life in a struggle with the authorities. His
blood lay hot on Menno's heart. His poor deluded brother was
man enough to die for what he thought was the truth, while
Menno knew the truth and did not follow it! A conscience-
stricken priest gave up to God in repentance that was deep and
sincere. He utterly yielded to Christ, and felt that he received
forgiveness, cleansing, and healing from his Lord. He seems for
about nine months to have remained in his Roman appointment,
no doubt hoping to lead his people to an evangelical faith and
experience. But on Sunday, January 30, 1536, he publicly renounced his Roman faith and post and turned to the peaceful
wing of the Melchiorites led by the devout and nonresistant
Obbe Philips. He was baptized by Obbe, and early in January
1537 he was ordained as an "Obbenite" elder by Obbe in the
Dutch province of Groningen.

Menno served his Anabaptist Brotherhood for twenty-five

years. For about seven years he seems to have labored in Holland, but about 1543 he turned to northwest Germany, especially the Rhineland. In 1546 he chose Holstein as his field of labor, and his final years were spent at Wuestenfelde, a village between Hamburg and Lübeck. Like Luther he took a wife soon after his conversion, a good woman named Gertrude who bore him a number of children. His son Jan seems to have died young, but he speaks of his daughters in 1558, and one of them became the mother of the wife of the martyrologist, Pieter Janz Twisck. Gertrude and Menno seem to have lived in wedded life for about twenty years before they were parted by her death. Menno was severely ill in January 1561. On the twenty-fifth anniversary of his renunciation of the Roman Church he roused himself on his sickbed and delivered a short exhortation to those present. The next day he passed away, January 31, 1561.

Menno Simons was the author of twenty-five books and booklets.[3] Undoubtedly his most influential treatise is the *Foundation of Christian Doctrine;* in Dutch, *Dat fundament des christelijken leers.* The 1558 edition was entitled *Een fundament en klare aanwijsinge* (A Foundation and Clear Instruction). The first part of the book is a vigorous call to real discipleship and includes discussions on repentance and faith. A major concern is the biblical doctrine of baptism. He also argues eloquently for religious toleration:

> Do not excuse yourselves, dear sirs, and judges, because you are the servants of the emperor. This will not clear you in the day of vengeance. It did not help Pilate that he crucified Christ in the name of the emperor. Serve the emperor in imperial matters, so far as Scripture permits, and serve God in divine matters. Then you may boast of His grace and have yourselves called after the Lord's name.
>
> Do not usurp the judgment and kingdom of Christ, for He alone is the ruler of the conscience, and besides Him there is no other. Let Him be your emperor in this matter and His holy Word your edict, and you will soon have enough of storming and slaying. You must hearken to God above the emperor, and obey God's Word more than that of the emperor.[4]

Menno described the true congregation of Christ as those who are truly converted, who are born from above of God, who are of a regenerate mind by the operation of the Holy Spirit through the hearing of the divine Word, and have become the children of God, have entered into obedience to Him, and live unblamably in His holy commandments, and according to His holy will all their days, or from the moment of their call.[5]

As to his own foundation he added:

> Brethren, I tell you the truth and lie not. I am no Enoch, I am no Elias, I am not one who sees visions, I am no prophet who can teach and prophesy otherwise than what is written in the Word of God and understood in the Spirit. (Whosoever tries to teach something else will soon leave the track and be deceived.) I do not doubt that the merciful Father will keep me in His Word so that I shall write or speak nothing but that which I can prove by Moses, the prophets, the evangelists and other apostolic Scriptures and doctrines, explained in the true sense, Spirit, and intent of Christ.[6]

This last phrase is the key to Menno's understanding of the Scriptures. All parts of God's Word witness to the Lord Jesus. Menno's motto was, "For no other foundation can anyone lay than that which is laid, which is Jesus Christ" (I Corinthians 3:11). Menno was a Christocentric churchman.

That Menno was a genuine evangelical is abundantly evident in his writings. In *Van 't rechte Christengeloove* (The True Christian Faith), about 1541, he fairly sings as he writes of Christ:

> Behold, my reader, such a faith . . . is the true Christian faith which praises, honors, magnifies, and extols God the Father and His Son Jesus Christ through loving fear and fearing love, for it recognizes the good will of the Father toward us through Christ. It recognizes, I say, that all the promises to the fathers, the expectation of the patriarchs, the whole figurative law, and all the prophecies of the prophets are fulfilled in Christ, with Christ, and through Christ. It acknowledges that Christ is our King, Prince, Lord, Messiah, the promised David, the Lion of the tribe of Judah, the strong One, the Prince of Peace, and the Father of the age to be; God's almighty, incomprehensible, eternal Word and Wisdom,

the firstborn of every creature, the Light of the world, the Sun of Righteousness, the True Vine, the Fountain of Life, the true Door and Shepherd of the sheep, the true Foundation and the precious Cornerstone in Zion, the right Way, the Truth, and Life, the promised Prophet, our Master and Teacher, our Redeemer, Saviour, Friend, and Bridegroom. In short, our only and eternal Mediator, Advocate, High Priest, Propitiator, and Intercessor; our Head and Brother.[7]

In his book, *Bericht van de Excommunicatie* (Account of Excommunication), 1550, Menno declared:

. . . I dare not go higher nor lower, be more stringent or lenient, than the Scriptures and the Holy Spirit teach me; and that out of great fear and anxiety of my conscience lest I once more burden the God-fearing hearts who now have renounced the commandments of men with more such commandments.[8]

On the role of the sacraments (baptism and Lord's Supper) Menno declared:

Faithful reader, do not imagine that we insist upon elements and rites. I tell you the truth in Christ and lie not. If anyone were to come to me, even the emperor or the king, desiring to be baptized, but walking still in the unclean, ungodly lusts of the flesh, and the unblamable, penitent, and regenerated life were not in evidence, by the grace of God, I would rather die than baptize such an impenitent, carnal person. For where there is no renewing, regenerating faith, leading to obedience, there is no baptism.[9]

Menno explained the meaning of grace in his book entitled, *Van 't rechte Christengeloove* (The True Christian Faith):

For all the truly regenerated and spiritually minded conform in all things to the Word and ordinances of the Lord. Not because they think to merit the atonement of their sins and eternal life. By no means. In this matter they depend upon nothing except the true promise of the merciful Father, given in grace to all believers through the blood and merits of Christ, which blood is and ever will be the only and eternal medium of our reconciliation; and not works, baptism, or the Lord's Supper . . . For if our reconciliation depended on

works and ceremonies, then grace would be a thing of the
past, and the merits and fruits of the blood of Christ would
end. Oh no, it is grace, and will be grace to all eternity; all
that the merciful Father does for us miserable sinners through
His beloved Son and Holy Spirit is grace. But reconciliation
takes place because men hear the voice of the Lord, believe
His Word, and therefore obediently observe and perform, although in weakness, the things represented by both signs
under water and bread and wine.[10]

In his booklet of about 1537 on regeneration, entitled *Van de
nieuwe creature* (The New Birth), Menno wrote a vigorous description of Christian holiness:

> The regenerate, therefore, lead a penitent and new life,
> for they are renewed in Christ and have received a new heart
> and spirit. Once they were earthly-minded, now heavenly;
> once they were carnal, now spiritual; once they were unright-
> eous, now righteous; once they were evil, now good, and
> they live no longer after the old corrupted nature of the first
> earthly Adam, but after the new upright nature of the new
> and heavenly Adam, Christ Jesus . . . Their poor, weak life
> they daily renew more and more, and that after the image of
> Him who created them. Their minds are like the mind of
> Christ, they gladly walk as He walked; they crucify and tame
> their flesh with all its evil lusts.[11]

Menno also stressed justification by faith. To a Christian
woman who was troubled by the depravity of her nature Menno
wrote a comforting letter about 1557, quoting many statements
from the Bible indicating that all the saints of history suffered in
the same way, and adding:

> Since it is plain from all these Scriptures that we must all
> confess ourselves to be sinners, as we are in fact; and since no
> one under heaven has perfectly fulfilled the righteousness
> required of God but Christ Jesus alone; therefore none can
> approach God, obtain grace, and be saved, except by the per-
> fect righteousness, atonement, and intercession of Jesus Christ,
> however godly, righteous, holy, and unblamable he may be.
> We must all acknowledge, whoever we are, that we are sinners
> in thought, word, and deed. Yes, if we did not have before

us the righteous Christ Jesus, no prophet nor apostle could be saved.[12]

On the other hand, Menno was most severe with those who tried to claim the promises of the gospel without living a holy life. In a harsh protest against the unvarnished sin of some professing Christians of the German Protestant state church he wrote this blast:

All they ask is that men say, Bah, what dishonorable knaves and scamps these confounded priests and monks are! The devil take them, the rascal pope with his shorn crew have deceived us long enough with their purgatory, confession, and fasting. We now eat whenever we get hungry, fish or flesh as we please, for every creature of God is good, says Paul, and nothing to be rejected. But what follows in Paul's statement they do not understand: namely, them which believe and know the truth and partake with thanksgiving. They say further, How miserably the priests have had us poor people by the nose, robbing us of the blood of the Lord, and directing us to their peddling and superstitious transactions. God be praised, we caught on that all our works avail nothing, but that the blood and death of Christ alone must cancel and pay for our sins. They strike up a Psalm, *Der Strick ist entzwei und wir sind frei*, etc. (Snapped is the cord, now we are free, praise the Lord) while beer and wine verily run from their drunken mouths and noses. Anyone who can but recite this on his thumb, no matter how carnally he lives, is a good evangelical man and a precious brother! If someone steps up in true and sincere love to admonish or reprove them for this, and point them to Christ Jesus rightly, to His doctrine, sacraments, and unblamable example, and to show that it is not right for a Christian so to boast and drink, revile and curse; then he must hear from that hour that he is one who believes in salvation by good works, is a heaven stormer, a sectarian agitator, a rabble rouser, a make-believe Christian, a disdainer of the sacraments, or an Anabaptist![13]

As a leading elder, Menno served as a sort of general superintendent in the Anabaptist Brotherhood, traveling about in North Germany, and sometimes visiting the Netherlands, aiding the local elders and strengthening the congregations in Christ. Although the Anabaptists stressed holiness of life, theirs was, of course, not a perfect church. Moral transgressions occurred which had to be dealt with. Other problems also arose. One of the elders, a man named Roelof Martens, but better known as Adam Pastor, became unsound in the Trinitarian faith; Pastor denied that Christ was eternal. The other leaders at first tried to lead Pastor back to evangelical faith in the Holy Trinity, but failing in this Menno Simons and Dirk Philips excommunicated Pastor in 1547. To counteract any erroneous influences which Pastor may have sowed in the Brotherhood, Menno wrote in 1550 his *Belijding van den drie eenigen en waren God* (Confession of the Triune God).

But the greatest danger to the Anabaptist fellowship was not heresy from within; it was persecution by the state, incited in many cases by the state-supported church clergy. Understandably this made the Anabaptists quite bitter against both the Catholic and Protestant leaders of the day. In a polemic against Jelle Smit, better known as Gellius Faber, of Emden in East Friesland, *Tegen Gillis Faber* (Reply to Gellius Faber), 1554, Menno wrote:

> He who purchased me with the blood of His love, and called me, who am unworthy, to His service, knows me, and He knows that I seek not wealth, nor possessions, nor luxury, nor ease, but only the praise of the Lord, my salvation, and the salvation of many souls. Because of this, I with my poor, weak wife and children have for eighteen years endured excessive anxiety, oppression, affliction, misery, and persecution. At the peril of my life I have been compelled everywhere to drag out an existence in fear. Yes, when the preachers repose on easy beds and soft pillows, we generally have to hide ourselves in out-of-the-way corners. When they at weddings and baptismal banquets revel with pipe, trumpet, and lute; we have to be on our guard when a dog barks for fear the arresting officer has arrived. When they are greeted as doctors, lords, and teachers by everyone, we have to hear that we are Anabaptists, bootleg preachers, deceivers, and heretics, and be saluted in the devil's name. In short, while they are gloriously rewarded for their services with large incomes and good times, our recompense and portion must be fire, sword, and death.[14]

In his book, *Vermaninge Van dat Lijden, Kruys, Vervolginge der Heyligen* (Admonition on the Suffering, Cross, and Persecution of the Saints) of about 1554, Menno protested the awful persecution which the Anabaptists then had to bear both in Catholic and Protestant lands:

> For how many pious children of God have we not seen during the space of a few years deprived of their homes and possessions for the testimony of God and their conscience; their poverty and sustenance written off to the emperor's insatiable coffers. How many have they betrayed, driven out of city and country, put to the stocks and torture? How many poor orphans and children have they turned out without a farthing? Some they have hanged, some have they punished with inhuman tyranny and afterward garroted them with cords, tied to a post. Some they have roasted and burned alive. Some, holding their own entrails in their hands, have powerfully confessed the Word of God still. Some they beheaded and gave as food to the fowls of the air. Some have they consigned to the fish. They have torn down the houses of some. Some have they thrust into muddy bogs. They have cut off the feet of some, one of whom I have seen and spoken to. Others wander aimlessly hither and yon in want, misery, and discomfort, in the mountains, in deserts, holes, and clefts of the earth, as Paul says. They must take to their heels and flee away with their wives and little children, from one country to another, from one city to another—hated by all men, abused, slandered, mocked, defamed, trampled upon, styled "heretics." Their names are read from pulpits and town halls; they are kept from their livelihood, driven out into the cold winter, bereft of bread, [and] pointed at with fingers. . . .[15]

In his *Brief Defense to All Theologians* of 1552, called in the Dutch, *Korte glaaglijke ontschuldiging* (Brief, Lamentable Apology), Menno made a list of ten topics on which he wished to participate in a theological disputation with the state churchmen: (1) The qualifications of evangelical preachers; (2) the unchangeable character of the doctrine of Christ and his Apostles; (3) Christ's perfect teaching, and his perfect sacrifice; (4) the source, nature, and fruit of regeneration; (5) Christian faith and love; (6) obedience to God's commandments; (7) Christian baptism; (8) the Lord's Supper; (9) ecclesiastical excommunication; and (10) the Christian life.[16]

No disputation of the type requested was ever granted Menno. A number of times he respectfully requested a disputation, with a guarantee of safe conduct, but his requests were always spurned. The clergy of Wesel in the land of Cleve replied that they preferred for the *Henker* (executioner) to treat with Menno! Somehow, in God's mercy, the hangman never did catch up with him, and he died a natural death at the age of sixty-five.

Leenaert Bouwens

The four most outstanding bishops or elders of the Anabaptists in the North were Menno, whose oversight covered the congregations from East Friesland to Holstein; Dirk Philips, who looked after the churches in Danzig and the Baltic area; Leenaert Bouwens, who served the congregations of Holland; and Gillis of Aachen (also known as Jelis of Aix-la-Chapelle), who served the Rhineland churches. Of these four men Menno was undoubtedly the most attractive personality and the most effective writer and leader. But we must not overlook the great gifts of Leenaert.

Leenaert Bouwens was born at Sommeldijk in 1515. Nothing is known of his family. During his youth he was a member of a club which was devoted to political oratory. After becoming an adult—by the time he was about thirty years of age—he was chosen as an Anabaptist preacher. In 1551 Menno ordained him to the office of elder. Leenaert's wife felt that she could hardly give her consent to his ordination, and she finally appealed to Menno himself to excuse her husband because of the great hazards of serving as an Anabaptist elder. Menno wrote her a tender reply, suggesting that she simply commit her husband into the sovereign care of God. Because of the great need of Leenaert's services in the Brotherhood, he did not find himself able to release him. The woman must have been persuaded, for Leenaert served long and well. He is best remembered as the elder who kept a name list of those whom he baptized in Holland. In five distinct periods from 1551 to 1582 he baptized no less than 10,252 persons. These lists are valuable in determining the times of founding and the early growth of some of the Dutch Mennonite congregations. Leenaert went through a period of difficulty—perhaps partly through unhappy relations with Dirk Philips in the middle 1560's—but after Dirk's death (1568) he resumed his office and baptized the last 3,509 persons of his career as bishop. He died a natural death at Hoorn in 1582, escaping the martyrdom which had loomed so large in the fears of his wife thirty years before.

Gillis

Gillis of Aachen was born around the year 1500 in the district of Jülich, which is now a part of the Dutch province of Limburg. At the trial of two Anabaptist women in 1540 a witness described Gillis as a pale man, of average height, with large eyes and a pointed brown beard. It is said that at times he wore his hair rather long, at other times short. No other Dutch leader is mentioned in testimonies of the martyrs as often as Gillis; he was the one who had baptized large numbers of them. He seems to have been involved in a moral lapse about the year 1552, but in 1554 he was reinstated to his office. The fall of Gillis was often used to reproach the early Dutch Anabaptists. In 1557 Gillis was captured, and on July 10 of that year he was to be burned as a heretic, as was generally the mode of execution for heretics in Catholic lands. Because of terror he recanted in an effort to avoid the fire. This did not save his life, but he was beheaded rather than burned to death. His right hand was also cut off, and his body was broken on the wheel. Gillis was the grandfather of Galenus Abrahamsz de Haan (1622-1706), a famous physician and Mennonite preacher and leader of Amsterdam.

Martyrdom Escaped

It is rather remarkable that of the four greatest leaders in the early history of the Dutch Anabaptists only Gillis died as a martyr. How closely these leaders may have come to apprehension and martyrdom we do not know. Menno reported in his *Reply to Gellius Faber,* 1554:

> About the year 1539, a householder who was a very pious man, named Tjaert Reynerdson, was seized in my stead, because out of compassion and love he had received me in his house secretly. He was a few days later put on the wheel after a free confession of faith, as a valiant knight of Christ, after the example of his Lord, although even his enemies testified that he was a pious man without reproach.
> Also, in 1546, at a place where they boast of the Word, a four-room house was confiscated, because the owner had rented one of the rooms for a short time, unknown to anybody, to my poor sick wife and her little ones.[17]

The early Dutch Mennonite martyrologist, P. J. Twisck, relates in his book, *Ondergangh der Tyrannen, en Jaerlijcksche Geschiedenisse* (Decline of the Tyrants, and Historical Incidents Year by Year), that he heard Menno's daughter (who was Twisck's mother-in-law) relate how on one occasion a certain traitor who personally knew Menno had agreed to identify him so as to bring about his capture. The traitor accompanied by officers was on a boat on a Dutch canal when a boat containing Menno passed theirs, going in the opposite direction. The traitor said nothing. Menno saw his danger, however, and leaped ashore after the boats passed, and escaped. After his escape the traitor spoke up and reported what had happened; he also explained that he had been unable to speak when he saw Menno. The authorities were so incensed that they put the would-be traitor to death.[18]

Professor N. van der Zijpp, the greatest living authority on Dutch Anabaptism, estimates the total number of Dutch Anabaptist martyrs at 2,500. The last one executed in the North was

Reyte Aysesz, who was put to death by drowning at Leeuwarden in Friesland on April 23, 1574. In the South the last martyr was Annaken van den Hove, who was buried alive on July 19, 1597, at Brussels in Flanders. Both martyrs were found by Catholic theologians to deserve death as heretics, and were handed over to the civil authorities of Friesland and Flanders respectively for execution.

III
ANABAPTISTS
AND THE BIBLE

✠

Basic Christian Doctrines

The original Anabaptists of Switzerland were evangelical believers on Christ who subscribed wholeheartedly to the Apostles' Creed. There was no doctrinal difference between them and Zwingli on such fundamental matters as the doctrine of God, the deity of Jesus Christ, the personality of the Holy Spirit, the sinful depravity of human nature, the doctrine of the new birth, or the personal return of Christ to raise the dead and judge the world. In the debate between the Swiss Brethren and the Reformed clergy, held at the Swiss town of Zofingen, some thirty miles west of Zurich, in 1532, the Reformed stated: "We are of one mind in the leading articles of faith, and our controversy has to do only with external things . . ." Zwingli himself commented: "But that no one may suppose that the dissension is in regard to doctrines which concern the inner man, let it be said that they make us difficulty only because of questions such as these: whether infants or adults should be baptized, and whether a Christian may be a magistrate." We may quote again the Strasbourg reformer, Wolfgang Capito, who stated: "As concerns the principal articles and vital points of faith, they do not err at all." Of course these sober and truthful evaluations were frequently denied in the heat of sixteenth-century polemics. A few generations later (1615), Johann Jacob Breitinger, head of the Zurich state church, asserted: "The Anabaptists have their peculiar ideas, but teach nevertheless faith in God, the Father, Son, and Holy Spirit. They do not hold errors which would cause a

57

man to be lost, but such as have been taught by some of the old church fathers."

Hymn Number 2 in the sixteenth-century Swiss Brethren hymnbook, the *Ausbund,* is entitled, "The Christian Faith in Metrical Form" (*Der Christliche Glaube, Gesangweise Gemacht*), and consists of a poetical arrangement of the Apostles' Creed with doctrinal comments. The hymn confesses faith in God and love for him who dwells in heaven, he who sees all our pains, who created all things, who is the Father of the pious, and who looks into the secrets of the heart. The hymn continues with faith in Christ the Saviour, "who is truly God's Son . . . born but not created, identical with the Father in being," born of a virgin, crucified under Pontius Pilate, buried, descended into Hades, resurrected on the third day, ascended to the Father's right hand, and will soon return (*Bald wird er wieder kommen*) to judge the wicked and the good, and to establish his eternal Kingdom. The hymn confesses faith in the Holy Spirit, God's secret power, who knows the thoughts of all hearts, who proceeds from the Father and the Son, and works life in us, the One whom we worship and to whom we render divine honor, who spoke through the prophets of the salvation which is now realized on earth through Christ who died. Finally the hymn turns to the fourth section of the creed and confesses faith in one holy, Apostolic church, which stands in the power of the Holy Spirit and allows him to work; one faith; one baptism by which we are washed from sin and united to God in a good conscience; one body; one Spirit; one Lord and God . . . who has called us to one hope, we who are now waiting for the promised salvation, when death shall be eternally captured and bound; all the dead who now are lying in the earth shall arise and precede us: the Lord knows their names. Finally, we believe in eternal life. The entire hymn is a ringing confession of the faith reflected in the Apostles' Creed. The Swiss Brethren would have been astonished and offended if they had been accused of not holding to a faith which is evangelical.

Some Doctrinal Issues

The main issues between Zwingli and the Anabaptists were these: (1) Ought the state church be maintained, or should a free church be set up? (2) Does the state have the right to maintain by law and force an established faith, or should liberty of conscience prevail? (3) Is the oath legitimate for Christians, or is it no longer permitted the people of God since the New Covenant was made by Christ? (4) Ought the infant baptism of the Roman Church be maintained, or should converts first be instructed, like the catechumens of the ancient church, and then baptized? (5) Are the principles of love and nonresistant suffering taught by Christ and the New Testament Apostles merely beautiful ideals which cannot always be followed literally, or are they basic and fundamental expressions of the new nature implanted in believers at their regeneration? (6) Does the Christian fulfill fundamentally dual roles in society, that of a solid citizen and that of a Christian disciple, so that as a Christian he may also serve in the magistracy and the military, or is society divided into two basically different groups: the church and the state, each with its own purpose, membership, function, method, ethic, and sanction? In each of these questions Zwingli chose the former alternative, while the Swiss Brethren felt that the latter was the proper Christian position. Since on each issue the Zurich Council agreed with Zwingli, nothing but persecution and continuous difficulty awaited the Anabaptists—in the sixteenth century this meant imprisonment and martyrdom—and continuing abuse through imprisonments, fines, confiscations, and even galley slavery as recently as a century or two later. Forcible baptisms of Mennonite children, as well as occasional imprisonment, continued in Bern until the nineteenth century.

Centrality of the Scriptures

The Anabaptists were devoted students of the Bible. From the moment of their conversion they became avid readers of

Scripture, memorizing favorite passages and preparing themselves to give biblical reasons for their faith. "I hope to be able to learn one hundred chapters of the Testament by heart," declared a sixteenth-century Anabaptist. The reason for this high evaluation of Scripture was of course the confidence that it was inspired by the Holy Spirit. In a sixteenth-century confession by the Anabaptists of Hesse, Article 1 declares:

> We believe, recognize, and confess that the Holy Scriptures both of the Old and New Testaments are to be described as commanded of God and written through holy persons who were moved thereto by the Spirit of God. For this reason the believing, born-again Christians are to employ them for teaching and admonishing, for reproof and reformation, to exhibit the foundation of their faith that it is in conformity with the Holy Scripture.

In the debate of 1532 at Zofingen the Swiss Brethren stated succinctly: "We hold that all things should be proved to ascertain what is founded on the Holy Word of God, for this will stand when heaven and earth pass away, as Christ Himself said." To his beloved friends and followers the imprisoned Swiss Brethren preacher, Michael Sattler, wrote in 1527: "And let no man remove you from the foundation which is laid through the letter of the holy Scriptures, and is sealed with the blood of Christ and of many witnesses of Jesus."

In the year 1544 a Dutch Anabaptist named John Claess was imprisoned at Amsterdam. To his wife and children he penned a number of memorial letters or "testaments." "Know, my dearly beloved wife," wrote John, "that it is my will and testament to you in no wise to depart from the word of the Lord . . ." And to his children he wrote: "My children, how you are to love God the Lord, how you must honor and love your mother, and love your neighbor, and fulfill all other commandments required of you by the Lord, the New Testament will teach you. . . . Whatever is not contained therein, believe not; but obey everything that is embraced in it." And again to his wife: "My dear wife, I request you to bring up my children in all good instruction, to have my testament read to them, and to bring them up in the Lord, according to your ability, as long as you remain with them." As he left the courtroom, following his death sentence, he cried out to the people present, "You citizens bear witness that we die for no other reason than for the true Word of God."[1] In 1550 a martyr named Hans Keeskooper wrote from a Ghent prison: "Therefore, search the Scriptures, which the Lord commands you to do, and to act according to them, on pain of the damnation of your souls, and of being cast into everlasting fire where there will be weeping and gnashing of teeth forever." In the same letter Keeskooper recorded the testimony of a boy who wished to join the Anabaptists but who had not yet been baptized.

"How came it," asked the civil lords, "that he did not baptize you?" The boy, "a mere lad yet, and a dear child," replied, "My lords, when the teacher presented the faith to me, and had interrogated me, he well perceived that I was still young in understanding, and bade me search the Scriptures still more; but I desired that it be done. He then asked me whether I knew that the world puts to death and burns such people. I replied, 'I know it well.' He then said to me, 'Hence, I pray you, that you have patience for this time, until I come another time. Search the Scriptures, and ask the Lord for wisdom, for you are yet a youth.' "

Keeskooper remarked, after writing this brief testimony, "See, dear friends, these are beautiful signs and miracles; open your eyes, and behold when such young persons give themselves for the truth, delivering their bodies into prison, and even unto death."[2]

Even a cursory reading of a few dozen interviews between the Roman clergy and Anabaptist prisoners will reveal the centrality of the Scriptures for the Brethren. The Anabaptists did not know much about the teachings of Augustine or Ambrose or Jerome, and were not at all impressed by citations from the ancient church fathers. Rather, they demanded definite statements from Scripture if they were to allow themselves to be "instructed." A French Anabaptist named Jacques D'Auchy was captured through the betrayal of a man of Harlingen in 1558 and imprisoned for many months at Leeuwarden in Friesland before being executed. He had long sessions with an inquisitor who hoped to return Jacques to the Roman faith. The inquisitor attacked as heretics and villains such Anabaptist leaders as Menno Simons, Leenaert Bouwens, and Gillis of Aachen. Jacques replied that he did not build his faith on men but on the Word of God. The inquisitor had with him a Latin Testament printed by Stephanus at Paris, as well as a Zurich German Testament. At first he would not allow Jacques the use of either, but finally he did permit Jacques to show him certain passages in the German Testament. The inquisitor insisted, however, that Jacques should not be guided by his own understandings but by those of Saints Augustine and Ambrose. Jacques, however, insisted on his right and his competence to read the Scriptures for himself. Jacques refused even to pay attention to the views of Menno Simons, although he probably agreed almost to a letter with him. It was the principle of *sola Scriptura* upon which he was clear; he would hearken to no human being so far as doctrinal truth was concerned; he had to see it in the Scriptures! The argument of the inquisitor that he was holding to a faith which was over 1,400 years old did not impress Jacques.

Jacques replied, "My lord, should I believe because of the long time? There were many heretics . . . who erred much longer yet. Turn to the Scriptures alone, according to the example of the good king Josiah." Jacques denied with vigor the right of the state to execute a man for wrong belief. The inquisitor cited Deuteronomy 13 as biblical proof that this was legitimate. Jacques replied that the law of Moses was not our guide, but the teaching of Christ: "What was commanded in the law is not commanded in the Gospel of Christ." Jacques then took the offensive by asking the inquisitor the meaning of Christ's proscription not to pull up the tares before the end of the world lest the wheat be pulled up also. The inquisitor replied that it is easy to see which is wheat and which is tares. "Yes, for Him that knows the seed," replied Jacques. To this the inquisitor assented.

Jacques then asked him point-blank whether he had the Spirit of God so as to know the things of the Spirit. He replied, "No, I will not answer this." Numerous examinations did not enhance the rapport of the two men, and the final chapter was written when Jacques was secretly put to death at night; he was found lying in his own blood, still wearing his leather clothes.[3] The ancient martyrologist added, "He now rests under the altar of Jesus, awaiting, with God's chosen, a blessed resurrection and eternal life."

Footwashing Observed Literally

It was because of their emphasis on recognizing no other authority at all that the Swiss Brethren and the Dutch Obbenites (later known as Mennists, Mennonists, Mennonites) did not build on dreams and visions, or any sort of private revelations. The Word of God alone, they declared, was sufficient for them. On the other hand, the principle of following the Bible strictly led some of the Dutch Anabaptists to adopt the practice of footwashing as a religious rite. Did not the Lord command the washing of one another's feet just as definitely as he instituted the ordinances of baptism and the communion of the Lord's Supper? Did not Christ say that he had given them an example, that they should do to one another as he had done to them? (John 13:1-17.) In his little book, *A Kind Admonition on Church Discipline,* 1541, Menno Simons wrote:

> Do wash the feet of your beloved brethren and sisters who are come to you from a distance, tired. Be not ashamed to do the work of the Lord, but humble yourselves with Christ, before your brethren, so that all humility of godly quality may be found in you.[4]

In a Dutch Mennonite Confession of Faith, drawn up at Amsterdam in 1627, we read:

> Feet washing we confess to be an ordinance of Christ which He Himself performed on His disciples, and after His ex-

ample commended to true believers . . . The purpose for which the Lord has instituted this ordinance is principally this: That we may remember in true humiliation that by grace we are washed from sin through the blood of Christ, and that He, our Lord and Master, by His lowly example binds us to true humility towards one another.[5]

Menno's colleague, Bishop Dirk Philips (c. 1504-1568), declared in his book, *The Church of God*, that Christ had two purposes in mind when he instituted the ordinance of footwashing:

> First, he would have us know that he himself must cleanse us after the inner man, and that we must allow him to wash away the sins which beset us . . . The second reason . . . is that we shall humble ourselves among one another . . . and that we hold our fellow-believers in the highest respect for the reason that they are the saints of God and members of the body of Jesus Christ, and that the Holy Ghost dwells in them.[6]

The Swiss Brethren, however, did not observe this command of Christ literally. In the year 1693 a major division occurred in the congregations of the Swiss Brethren. The division began in the canton of Bern and spread to the congregations in Alsace and in the Rhenish Palatinate. The occasion for the tension was the attempt of a young bishop named Jacob Ammann to introduce the Dutch practice of *shunning* excommunicated members (which Obbe Philips had inaugurated to protect his Brotherhood from the dangerous fanaticism of the Münsterites). Ammann felt that shunning was a biblical command (I Corinthians 5:11). An older Swiss bishop, Hans Reist, vigorously opposed Ammann, insisting that the verses cited on not eating with an impenitent church member applied primarily to the Lord's Supper. The outcome of the controversy, in which personal attitudes certainly played a role, was the only major division in the history of the congregations of Anabaptist background in Switzerland. Following this rupture in fellowship in 1693 the followers of Ammann, who are even today called "Amish" in America, began to keep footwashing as a religious rite. But the Reist congregations maintained the earlier Swiss Brethren attitude of seeing in John 13:1-17 an object lesson in love and brotherhood among Christians, rather than the institution of a ceremony for the church to observe literally.

Attitude Toward the Old Testament

Finally we must look carefully at the most distinctive theological emphasis of the Anabaptists. It concerns their view of the relation of the Old Testament to the New. Actually, Christendom as a whole has never been entirely clear on this question. One of the best Protestant expositions is that of John Calvin in his *Institutes of the Christian Religion,* Book II, Chapter xi, where he shows how the Christian is delivered from the ceremonial law of Moses, and how Christ has brought deeper inward spiritual blessings than the Old Covenant saints enjoyed. But the Anabaptists went further. They thought it was not legitimate to argue, as did the leading Reformers of the sixteenth century, that because oaths and warfare were commanded or permitted in the Old Covenant, that Christians may therefore employ them today. The Reformers emphasized the unity of the two covenants, thought the Anabaptists, in order to justify infant baptism by a comparison with circumcision, to plead the legitimacy of the magistracy and the oath, and perhaps even to justify the persecution of religious dissenters from the Old Testament! By contrast, the Anabaptists stressed the preparatory role of the Old Testament; it was, they declared, one of shadows and types, while the reality is in Christ. God tolerated such things as divorce, the oath, and the like, because of the "hardness of heart" of Israel, but such concessions no longer apply. (No Anabaptist could have signed a statement that it was permissible for Philip of Hesse to have two wives because Abraham did! In fairness to the Reformers who did sign such a statement, it should be added that they did so with hesitation and regret, feeling almost compelled to do so because of the crucial necessity of maintaining the good will of Philip, Landgrave of Hesse. This crisis would have been one more consideration militating against the whole state church system, so far as the Anabaptists were concerned.) The teachings of Christ and the Apostles, declared the Anabaptists, fulfilled the Old Testament. That is, the New Testament seizes upon those elements which were permanent and valid in the Old Testament, and builds upon them, while it sloughs off (by silence, generally) those things in the Old Testament which are not a part of God's final and perfect revelation in Christ.

In a brief treatise entitled, *The Tabernacle of Moses,* Dirk Philips wrote:

> So then the gospel and the law are divided, so far as the figures, shadows and the letter of the law are concerned, which are all done away by the gospel. But it is essential that we take heed to the spirit of the law, (for the law is spiritual), as Paul says . . . We will then find that the signification, purport and real meaning of the law accords and agrees in every way with the gospel, yea, that it is one and the same truth. . . . Thus the literal command of the Lord regarding circumcision of the flesh has come to an end, but the command regarding the spiritual circumcision of the heart remains.[7]

And in his book, *Spiritual Restitution,* Dirk declared:

> The false prophets . . . embellish and disguise their deceptive doctrine with the old leaven of the letter as shadows and figures; for whatever of the new testament they cannot defend they try to prove with the old testament . . . From this fallacy many sects have come, [and] many false forms of worship have been established. . . .[8]

In a sharp blast against the "corrupt sects" of the sixteenth century (Davidians, Münsterites, and Batenburgers), Menno wrote in his *Foundation of Christian Doctrine:*

> If you want to appeal to the literal understanding and transactions of Moses and the prophets, then must you also become Jews, accept circumcision, possess the land of Canaan literally, erect the Jewish kingdom again, build the city and temple, and offer sacrifices and perform the ritual as required in the law. And you must declare that Christ the promised Saviour has not yet come, He who has changed the literal

and sensual ceremonies into new, spiritual, and abiding realities.[9]

In reference to the notion that Elijah must yet come, Menno continued:

> Even though Elijah himself were to come, he would not have anything to teach contrary to the foundation and doctrine of Christ and the apostles. But he must teach and preach in harmony with them if he would execute the office of the true preacher, for by the Spirit, Word, actions, and example of Christ, all must be judged until the last judgment. . . . For Christ is the man who sits upon David's throne and shall reign forever in the kingdom, house, and congregation of Jacob.[10]

In *The True Christian Faith* (about 1541), Menno wrote in the same vein: "The true evangelical faith sees and considers only the doctrine, ceremonies, commands, prohibitions, and the perfect example of Christ, and strives to conform thereto with all its power."[11]

Pilgram Marpeck (d. 1556), the "Menno Simons of the South," an Anabaptist elder who labored in South Germany and Switzerland, wrote an entire book contrasting the Old Covenant with the New; it was called the *Testament Explanation*. Only two copies are known today, one in the Zentralbibliothek of Zurich, the other in Marburg, Germany.

It would not be correct to say that the Anabaptists had a low view of the Old Testament. On the contrary, they held that the entire Bible was inspired and profitable for doctrine. It was rather that they rejected the concept of a "flat Bible." They took the principle of progressive revelation seriously, holding that the New Testament is God's perfect and final revelation, and that the Old Testament was in God's intention preparatory in character. They believed that in this view they were true both to the letter and to the spirit of the New Testament.

IV

THE CHURCH
AND THE SACRAMENTS

✠

The doctrine of the church stood at the center of Anabaptist thought. The Brethren regarded the church as the final goal of all of God's redemptive acts in history. No other institution will ever displace the church. It is nothing less than the glorious Kingdom of the Messiah prophesied in the Old Testament. They regarded the church as the fellowship of the saints, the Body of Christ, the Brotherhood of the redeemed, the society in which the Spirit of Christ is at work transforming men into the spiritual image of Jesus, the Body of which Christ is Head, and where his will for men is carried out, "albeit in human weakness."

A Free Church

First of all, declared the Anabaptists, the church must be free. What is taken for granted in America today, however, was regarded as rank heresy in the sixteenth century. The very worst offense of the Anabaptists was their challenge of the inclusive membership and state establishment of the church. How in the name of all that is holy and reasonable, the state churchmen asked, could anyone dare to defy the *corpus Christianum,* the sacred union of church and state that reached clear back to the joint edict of Theodosius the Great and Gratianus (A.D. 380)? Such a heresy as wishing to throw wide open the whole matter of faith, and to allow the church to find its own way without the benefit of a co-operating state, must be punished with nothing less than death. Such views would simply wreck the established order and introduce chaos into a well-ordered society!

The Anabaptists quietly insisted that they had no choice but to follow the Word of God. The church of the New Testament era was a free church, said the Anabaptists. It did not link hands with the state and secure legal recognition. Much less did it call on the secular government to maintain the true faith by law, and to punish dissenters with martyrdom! Christ is the only Lord of the conscience, asserted the Anabaptists, and only those who freely accept Christ and become converted are qualified for membership in the Body of Christ.

In a brief booklet of 1539 entitled, *Why I Do Not Cease Teaching and Writing,* Menno explained:

> They verily are not the true congregation of Christ who merely boast of His name. But they are the true congregation of Christ who are truly converted, who are born from above of God, who are of a regenerate mind by the operation of the Holy Spirit through the hearing of the divine Word, and have become the children of God, have entered into obedience to Him, and live unblamably in His holy commandments, and according to His holy will all their days, or from the moment of their call.[1]

Freedom of Conscience

Involved in this program for a free church was, of course, the matter of voluntarism in matters of faith and full religious toleration. The proper business of the magistrate, insisted the Anabaptists, was to encourage the good and punish the evil; or—to use a modern expression—to maintain law and order. No one ought to be harmed for following the Word of God as he understood it. And yet the Anabaptists were being destroyed in great numbers because they wished to set up congregations of earnest disciples who desired only to follow Christ in holiness and obedience.

In his book, *Christian Baptism,* 1539, Menno wrote to the civil authorities:

> Take heed, ye illustrious, noble, and reverend sirs. Take heed, ye who enforce the laws in the country against whom it

is that your cruel, bloody sword is sometimes sharpened and drawn. . . .

Therefore we pray you, as our beloved and gracious rulers according to the flesh, by the mercy of God, to consider and realize if there be reasonableness in you, in what great anxiety and anguish we poor, miserable people are placed. If we abandon Christ Jesus and His holy Word, we fall into the wrath of God. And if we remain firm in His holy Word, then we are put to your cruel sword.[2]

In 1550 a Dutch Anabaptist named Hans van Overdam submitted a lengthy epistle to the civil authorities which reads in part:

Be it known to you, noble lords, councilors, burgomasters, and judges, that we recognize your offices as right and good; yea, as ordained and instituted of God, that is, the secular sword for the punishment of evil-doers and the protection of the good, and we desire to obey you in all taxes, tributes, and ordinances, as far as it is not contrary to God. And if you find us disobedient in these things, we will willingly receive our punishment as malefactors. God, who is acquainted with every heart, knows that this is our intention.

But understand, ye noble lords, that the abuse of your stations or offices we do not recognize to be from God but from the devil, and that antichrist through the subtlety of the devil has bewitched and blinded your eyes . . . Be sober, therefore, and awake, and open the eyes of your understanding, and see against whom you fight, that it is . . . against God.

Therefore we will not obey you; for it is the will of God that we shall be tried thereby. Hence we would rather, through the grace of God, suffer our temporal bodies to be burned, drowned, beheaded, racked, or tortured, as it may seem good to you, or be scourged, banished, or driven away, and robbed of our goods, than show you any obedience contrary to the Word of God, and we will be patient herein, committing vengeance to God.[3]

No Sacramentalism

It was the church that was central for the Anabaptists, not ceremonies. Baptism, for example, played a secondary role in

Anabaptist thought. "If you are a genuine Christian born of God, then why do you draw back from baptism, which is the least that God has commanded you?" asked Menno in his *Foundation of Christian Doctrine*.[4] He continued by setting forth God's demands for holiness of heart and life, and readiness to suffer as his disciple. Then he added, "It seems to me that these and the like commands are more painful and difficult for perverse flesh, naturally so prone to follow its own way everywhere, than to be the recipient of a handful of water. . . . Faithful reader, do not imagine that we insist upon elements and rites."[5]

It would appear understandable that the Protestant theologians should have arrived at precisely this same conclusion after they had once been delivered from the sacramentalism of the Roman Church. And this was actually the conclusion of Zwingli in 1523, for he wrote to a friend on June 15, "It is useless to wash a thousand times in the baptismal water him who does not believe." And the next year, on October 20, 1524, Zwingli wrote, "God has commanded to baptize those who have previously believed." But after the battle with the free church *Täufer* was on, Zwingli defended infant baptism vigorously.

For the Anabaptists the important factor was not the outward water baptism but the inner "baptism" of the Holy Spirit, the spiritual change effected by Christ through the Spirit in those who turned from sin to become his disciples.

Thomas von Imbroich was a young Anabaptist bishop, twenty-five years of age. His native village was Imgenbroich, not far from Aachen. He moved to Cologne in 1554 and united with the Brethren. Soon he was chosen to the ministry, and served briefly before his early martyrdom as an elder or bishop in the Brotherhood. He was imprisoned at Cologne, Germany, in December 1557. His arrest took place December 23, 1557. He was repeatedly examined, cruelly tortured, and finally beheaded on March 5, 1558. In prison he wrote a brief confession of faith for the judges of the Inquisition, and a copy was smuggled out to the Brethren, who promptly had it printed. He also wrote letters to his wife and to the church. These materials were later assembled and published in a book with the curious title, *Güldene Aepfel in Silbern Schalen* (Golden Apples in Silver Bowls).

> I believe and confess [wrote Thomas] that there is a Christian baptism which must take place externally and internally; internally with the Holy Ghost and with fire, externally with water in the name of the Father, the Son, and the Holy Ghost. Internal baptism is imparted by Christ to the penitent, as John the Baptist said: "I indeed baptize you with water unto repentance: but He that cometh after me is mightier than I; whose shoes I am not worthy to bear; He shall baptize you with the Holy Ghost and with fire. . . ."
>
> But the external baptism of water, which is a witness of the spiritual baptism, and indication of true repentance, and a sign of faith in Jesus Christ, is administered by the command of the Almighty Father and His Son Jesus Christ and the Holy Ghost, and in the name of the only God . . . to those who have repented and reformed, believe the Gospel, confess their faith and desire baptism, willingly offer themselves up to God, and yield themselves servants unto righteousness, yea, to the service of God and the communion of Jesus Christ and all the saints.
>
> This is fully comprehended and contained in the words which Christ speaks to His disciples: "Go ye therefore and teach all nations, baptizing them in the name of the Father, and of the Son, and of the Holy Ghost: teaching them to observe all things whatsoever I have commanded you." . . . In Mark we read thus: "Go ye into all the world and preach the Gospel to every creature. He that believeth and is baptized shall be saved; but he that believeth not shall be damned. . . .
>
> These words of Christ fully comprise the ordination and institution of the Christian baptism, and all that pertains to it; for Christ who is the eternal Wisdom of the Father has expressly and completely thus commanded it. Now as He is the Light and the Saviour of the world we find in this command that teaching and believing must precede baptism. . . .
>
> The Scriptures cannot be broken, neither are we to take away from or add to the Word of God; nay, not even the smallest tittle or letter of the Gospel may be changed. Hence the ordinance of the Lord respecting baptism must remain unaltered, for it is the Word of God which abideth forever. . . .

Hence, the words of Christ declare that teaching must take place before and after baptism in order that the person baptized may use diligence to observe after baptism the Gospel (which was presented to him before baptism) and all things commanded him; for he is no more lord over himself; but as a bride surrenders herself to her bridegroom, so he after receiving baptism surrenders himself to Christ and loses his will, is resigned in all things, without name [status], without will, but leaving the name to Christ and letting Him reign in him. For this is the signification of baptism, that the Christian's life is nothing but pure dying and suffering; because we are like unto the image of Christ, and baptized with Him, must die and suffer, if we would reign and live with Him.[6]

Spiritual Status of Children

As to the salvation of unbaptized children, Thomas referred to the promise of Matthew 19:14: "Let the children come to me, and do not hinder them; for to such belongs the kingdom of heaven."

We believe and confess that infants are saved on account of the promise; but that salvation depends on baptism we do not confess; for when Christ promised the children the kingdom of God they were not baptized, nor did He baptize them, but He embraced them, and spoke kindly to or blessed them. . . . Hence, since we are admonished to become as children, it is incontrovertible that as long as they remain in a state of innocence God holds them guiltless and no sin is imputed to them. And although they are of a sinful nature, partaking of the nature of Adam, there still remains something in them which is pleasing to God, namely innocence and humility. However they are saved only through the grace of Christ. . . .

Who will accuse the children for whom Christ shed His blood? Who will condemn them to whom Christ has promised the kingdom of God? Who will deny the holy Scriptures which declare so emphatically that the sin of Adam and of the whole world has been taken away? . . . Hence, he who says that children are condemned, or accuses them on account of original sin, denies the death and blood of Christ. For if the children are condemned because of Adam's death, then Christ died in vain, Adam's guilt is still upon us and not reconciled through Christ, and grace has not abounded over sin through Christ. God forbid![7]

Menno Simons, in his book entitled *Christian Baptism*, 1539, wrote:

> But little children and particularly those of Christian parentage have a peculiar promise which was given them of God without any ceremony, but out of pure and generous grace through Jesus Christ our Lord who says, "Suffer little children, and forbid them not, to come unto me; for of such is the kingdom of heaven." Matt. 19:14; Mark 10:14; Luke 18:16. This promise makes glad and assures all the chosen saints of God in regard to their children or infants. By it they are assured that the true word of our beloved Lord Jesus Christ could never fail. Inasmuch as He has shown such great mercy toward the children that were brought to Him that He took them up in His blessed arms, blessed them, laid His hands upon them, promised them the kingdom of heaven, and has done no more with them; therefore such parents have in their hearts a sure and firm faith in the grace of God concerning their beloved children, namely that they are children of the kingdom, of grace, and of the promise of eternal life through Jesus Christ our Lord (to whom alone be the glory) and not by any ceremony. Yes, by such promise they were assured that their dear children, as long as they are mere children, are clean, holy, saved, and pleasing unto God, be they alive or dead. Therefore they give thanks to the eternal Father through Jesus Christ our Lord for His inexpressibly great love to their dear children, and they train them in the love of God and in wisdom by correcting, chastising, teaching, and admonishing them, and by the example of an irreproachable life, until these children are able to hear the Word of God, to believe it, and to fulfill it in their works. Then is the time, and not until then, of whatever age they may be, that they should receive Christian baptism, which Christ Jesus has commanded in obedience to His Word to all Christians, and which His apostles have practiced and taught.[8]

The Lord's Supper

There was no controversy at all between the Reformed and the Anabaptists on the nature of the Lord's Supper. Both groups regarded the emblems as symbols of Christ's broken body and

shed blood, which was the teaching of Zwingli. The major con-
troversies which involved the Anabaptists were those relating to
the Roman Catholic doctrines of transubstantiation and communion in one kind, and to the lack of discipline in the Lutheran
territorial churches, a practice which resulted in the indiscrimi-
nate serving of the bread and the cup to those who were living
carelessly in sin and who nevertheless presented themselves as
communicants at the Table of the Lord.

In 1549 a young woman named Elizabeth Dirks was arrested
at Leeuwarden in Friesland. She was interrogated in the town
hall by the members of the council. These councilmen were
Roman Catholics. Following is part of the record of the examination.

> *Lords:* "What are your views with regard to the most ador-
> able, holy sacrament?"
> *Elizabeth:* "I have never in my life read in the holy Scrip-
> tures of a holy sacrament, but of the Lord's Supper. . . ."
> *Lords:* "Be silent, for the devil speaks through your
> mouth."
> *Elizabeth:* "Yea, my lords, this [charge] is a small matter,
> for the servant is not better than his lord."
> *Lords:* "You speak from a spirit of pride."
> *Elizabeth:* "No, my lords, I speak with frankness."
> *Lords:* "What did the Lord say, when He gave His disciples
> the Supper?"
> *Elizabeth:* "What did He give them, flesh or bread?"
> *Lords:* "He gave them bread."
> *Elizabeth:* "Did not the Lord remain sitting there? Who
> then would eat the flesh of the Lord?"[9]

The interrogation then proceeded to other points of Catholic
doctrine, only to be continued further at a later hearing. In the
final analysis, she was executed by drowning on May 27, 1549.
She may have been the first deaconess of the Dutch Mennonites
(a deaconess was a woman set apart for the pastoral care of
women and girls in the church). Hymn 13 in the Anabaptist
hymnbook, the *Ausbund,* is devoted to the story of her testimony
and death.

As to the Catholic doctrine of the Lord's Supper, Menno Simons wrote:

> They have made the bread in the Holy Supper into the actual flesh, and the wine into the actual blood, of Christ, and that by virtue of Christ's Word taken literally: "Take, eat; this is my body." They fail to notice that John says in John 6 (where he instructs us plainly how we are to eat His flesh and drink His blood) that it is useless to eat His flesh literally and to drink His blood. Nor could it be done, because He was about to ascend to the place where He was before; therefore we are not to understand this eating His flesh and drinking His blood literally but spiritually. As He Himself says, "The words that I speak unto you, they are spirit, and they are life." All those who confess this from the Scriptures (by many disdainfully called cursed heretics and profaners of the sacrament) must suffer for it by water, fire, and the sword.[10]

In two brief summary statements on the sacraments, Menno wrote:

> And these are the sacraments which Christ Jesus has instituted and taught. First, the holy baptism of believers in which we bury our sinful flesh and take unto ourselves a new life, seal and confess our faith, testify to the new birth and a good conscience, and enter into the obedience of Jesus Christ . . . Second, the Holy Supper in which is represented the death of the Lord who died for us in His great love, and in which is represented true, brotherly love, and also the righteous, unblamable Christian life which must be lived inwardly and outwardly in full measure of death unto sin and unfeigned love, comformable to the Word of God.[11]
>
> It is not the sacraments nor the signs, such as baptism and the Lord's Supper, but a sincere, Christian faith, with its unblamable, pious fruits, represented by the sacraments, that makes a true Christian and has the promise of life.[12]

Menno was also quite indignant against communion "in one kind" as practiced in the Catholic Church. At least twice in his writings he makes mention of the wrongful withholding of the cup from the laity.

Truly, I do not know how a worse heresy could be invented, notwithstanding that these miserable men cruelly cry against us, saying, "Heretics! heretics! Drown them, slay them, and burn them!" And this for no other reason than that we teach the new life, baptism on confession of faith, and the Supper in both elements in an unblamable church, according to the holy Gospel of Christ Jesus.[13]

For Menno, one of the most distressing situations in the sixteenth century was the offering of the Lord's Supper to the rank and file of the population, all of whom were recognized as good Christians because they had been christened, and because they partook of the Lord's Supper, although their church required neither faith nor holiness as conditions for being communicant members. "Of the Supper of the preachers," wrote Menno in one of his sharp polemical attacks on the state churchmen,

we hold and confess, first, that it is a false and idolatrous consolation and symbol of peace to those who delight in walking upon the broad way, such as the greedy, avaricious, usurers, the adulterers, the lying, deceiving, proud, and unrighteous. It is praised to them by their preachers that the remission of their sins is announced thereby. Therefore they console themselves and think that if they partake of it, they are the people of the Lord. Oh, no! The ceremony makes no Christian, for so long as they do not become converted and do not become new men, born of God, of [a] spiritual mind, all baptizing and partaking of the Lord's Supper is meaningless, even if it were administered by Peter or Paul.[14]

In a severe tone Menno declared:

The Lutherans teach and believe that faith alone saves, without any assistance by works. They emphasize this doctrine so as to make it appear as though works were not even necessary; yes, that faith is of such a nature that it cannot tolerate any work alongside of it. And therefore the important and earnest epistle of James (because he reproves such a frivolous, vain doctrine and faith) is esteemed and treated as a "strawy epistle." What bold folly! If the doctrine is straw, then the chosen apostle, the faithful servant and witness of Christ who wrote and taught it, must also have been a strawy man. . . .[15]

Restoration of the Apostolic Church

The Anabaptists had a deep conviction that the ancient church started out well but rapidly declined in purity of doctrine and in spiritual power, especially in the fourth century when toleration came, when the church began to link hands with the rulers of this world, and when Christianity was finally made the state religion of the Roman Empire (A.D. 380). The Brethren therefore were not content to remove a few obvious corruptions in the Roman Church of the sixteenth century. They thought Zwingli was on the right track when he decided to abolish whatever in the church was not taught in the Scriptures. But they held that Zwingli did not consistently carry out this principle; they felt that he did not go far enough. They were determined to return fully to the apostolic church of the New Testament for their model. They had a strong sense that the Anabaptist Brotherhood was a restoration of primitive Christianity, that their reformation was a genuine restitution of the New Testament church. To take only one writer, this strain runs through all of Menno Simons' writings.

In the preface to a later edition of his *Foundation* of 1539, Menno commented:

> I perceive that our work which I published a few years ago under the title, *Foundation of Christian Doctrine,* has through the grace of God (to whom be eternal praise and thanks) been productive of much good to some. God's holy Word which was obscured for such a long time has through our little talent been brought back to light.[16]

And near the end of this book he added:

> Behold, beloved sirs, friends, and brethren, here you have the leading parts and chief articles of a Christian position or system, together with a plain instruction and exposition of the anti-Christian abominations and Babylonian traffic by which the true apostolic truth, because of the long time, was wiped out and demolished.[17]

In his book, *Christian Baptism,* Menno labeled the Bible doctrine which he had set forth, "this heavenly truth of Christ," and described it as "for so many ages lost and now regained."[18] In *The True Christian Faith,* about 1541, he became oratorical:

> Again I say, reform! Too long you have erred; too long you have mocked God; too long you have worshiped Antichrist instead of Christ; too long you have walked in the perverse and broad way of death. Awaken, it is yet today! Behold, the true book of the Law, the saving, pure Gospel of Christ which was hid for so many centuries by the abominations of Antichrist, has been found![19]

In his *Confession of the Distressed Christians,* 1552, he declared,

> The brightness of the sun has not shone for many years; heaven and earth have been as copper and iron; the brooks and springs have not run, nor the dew descended from heaven; the beautiful trees and verdant fields have been dry and wilted—spiritually, I mean. However, in these latter days the gracious, great God by the rich treasures of His love has again opened the windows of heaven and let drop the dew of His divine Word, so that the earth once more as of yore produces its green branches and plants of righteousness which bear fruit unto the Lord and glorify His great and adorable name. The holy Word and sacraments of the Lord rise up again from the ashes by means of which the blasphemous deceit and abominations of the learned ones are made manifest. Therefore all the infernal gates rouse themselves, they rave and rant and with such subtle deceit, blasphemous falsehood, and bloody tyranny that if the strong God did not show forth His gracious power, no man could be saved. But they will never wrest from Him those that are His own.[20]

And in his *Instruction on Excommunication,* 1558, Menno exclaimed,

> We see all this and observe that now the bright light of the holy Gospel of Christ shines again in undimmed splendor in these latest awful times of anti-Christian abominations. God's only-begotten and firstborn Son, Jesus Christ, is gloriously revealed; His gracious will and holy Word concerning

faith, regeneration, repentance, baptism, the Lord's Supper, and the whole saving doctrine, life, and ordinance have again come to light through much seeking and prayer; through action, reading, teaching, and writing. Now all things (God be praised for His grace) proceed according to the true apostolic rule and criterion in the church, by which the kingdom of Christ comes to honor and the kingdom of Antichrist is going down in shame.[21]

Society Must Be Evangelized

The Anabaptists saw as the major function of the church the evangelism of all men with the gospel. This position they based on such statements of Christ as "Go therefore and make disciples of all nations" (Matthew 28:19), "As the Father has sent me, even so I send you" (John 20:21), and "You shall be my witnesses in Jerusalem and in all Judea and Samaria and to the end of the earth" (Acts 1:8).

The ancient Christian church did a remarkable work in carrying the gospel over the then-known world in the first century without the benefit of modern travel facilities or trained personnel; the happy witnesses simply told the Good News as they moved about in daily concourse with their fellows, and the light of Christianity spread rapidly across Europe and North Africa. This took place in spite of severe persecution, even Empire-wide in extent at times, especially in the reigns of Decius in the middle of the third century, and of Diocletian early in the fourth century. Constantine's Edict of Toleration had come in A.D. 313, and on February 28, 380, by a joint edict of Theodosius, the Eastern Emperor, and of Gratianus, the Western Emperor, Christianity became the official state religion of the Empire. From that date it was a crime not to be Christian! Infants were "made Christians" (christened) by baptism, and Europe gradually settled into the comfortable status of consciously being no longer pagan but Christian, for were not all citizens members of the great universal or catholic church? Long before the time of the Reformation the baptism of infants had become universal and all Europeans were thought of as Christians. Not all of them were pious in life, of course, but what of it? And no matter that some of the clergy were also somewhat carnal. For did not the grace of God operate through the seven sacraments regardless of the character of the officiating priest, and were not many of the most unspiritual prelates of the church after all excellent rulers? How could there be any thought of evangelism in such a satisfactory arrangement?

And yet all was not well. Somehow the gospel had lost its clarity in this institutionalized Christendom. Many devout Christian thinkers in various lands—Waldo, Wycliffe, Hus, Luther, Zwingli—labored to cleanse the church of its obvious abuses and to restore the great truths of the gospel: justification by faith alone, the Christian life as one of holiness and obedience to God's Word, the church as the fellowship of the redeemed, the priesthood of all believers, the sufficiency and clarity of Scripture as a spiritual guide, the headship of Jesus Christ over the church, prayer to God only. In 1517 Martin Luther inaugurated a glorious reformation which enabled the church to discard compulsory fasts, the required celibacy of the clergy, the institution of popery, the twin doctrines of indulgences and purgatory, the use of images and relics, the Roman doctrine of Tradition (whereby all nonbiblical practices and doctrines were justified as apostolic), all notions of human merit, the doctrine of the Mass as a bloodless repetition of Calvary. The debt of modern Christendom to Luther for the inaugurations of the sixteenth century is simply enormous. God used him mightily to recover the truth of the gospel and to purify the church of the unscriptural accretions of more than a millennium of time.

The doctrine of evangelism was not recovered adequately by the Reformers, however. They labored manfully to restore biblical Christianity to Europe, and they did not hesitate to link hands with the secular rulers to carry through their reforms. But they never reached the point of setting up free churches of voluntary members. The *corpus Christianum* was reformed but retained. Luther regretfully set up what he called the *landesherr-*

liche Kirchenregiment, a system of territorial churches in which the civil ruler of each territory determined the faith of his realm. Every priest and layman then had to change his faith to that of the ruler, or migrate to another land on pain of persecution. The *corpus Christianum* was badly broken from one land to another, but it survived through the state church system which enforced conformity to the established religion in each country.

Against this entire program the Anabaptists protested bitterly. The Reformation which they hailed initially with great joy was to them in its later development a keen disappointment. In the polemical style of that era they accused the Reformers of failing to go all the way with a biblical reformation, and even of being the second beast of Revelation 13! They were particularly bitter when Catholic and Lutheran and Reformed rulers set about to crush the Anabaptist free-church movement by fines, confiscations of property, banishment, imprisonment, torture, and martyrdom.

The Anabaptists first of all looked at the moral and spiritual level of the populations about them and pronounced them as for the most part in need of evangelism. Such people are not born again, they declared; they are lost. They imagine that they are Christians because as infants they were baptized but they give no evidence of new life in Christ. "They console themselves," declared Thomas von Imbroich, "only with this, namely, 'I am a Christian; for I am baptized.' Thus they speak, thinking that it is sufficient if one is only baptized; but they know little what baptism signifies. For they have not yet drank of the living fountain. . . ."

In the second place, the Anabaptists denied the right of any ruler to determine the faith of his subjects. For them, only Christ was the Lord of the conscience.[22] No man dared to step into the sacred realm of faith to specify what other men should believe, be he judge, ruler, king, or emperor. The Anabaptists wanted to follow the Scriptures as closely as God gave them grace. But in attempting to do so they ran straight into the hands of the law, for Anabaptism was made a capital crime in one land after another.[23] In his *Foundation* Menno protested to the civil authorities:

> But the reviling, betraying, and agitation of the priests and your unmerciful mandates and edicts must be our scriptures, and your rackers, hangmen, wrath, torture chambers, water and stake, fire and sword (O God) must be our instructors and teachers, to whom we sorrowful children must listen in many places, and finally make good with our possessions and lifeblood. . . . This I know for certain, that all bloodthirsty preachers and all rulers who propose and practise these things are not Christ's disciples. The hour of accounting when you depart this life will teach you the truth.[24]

Finally, the Anabaptists declared that no ruler had the right to hinder the free teaching of God's Word. Since the whole state church system was an unscriptural and unfortunate arrangement, so far as they were concerned, they cared nothing at all for any sort of state recognition of their clergy. Indeed, although they did choose and ordain deacons, preachers, and elders (bishops), they made little difference between the ordained and the unordained; all members were expected to be born-again witnesses of Jesus Christ, authorized by him to tell the Good News of salvation from sin through Jesus Christ. Because of their doctrine of nonresistance they tended to arouse suspicion when they traveled without arms, especially without the common sword or rapier. Then when they refused to set up drinks in inns, and when they ventured to speak a word to a stranger about the salvation of his soul, and when they bowed their heads in silent prayer at the beginning and end of their meals, someone was sure to summon the authorities with the report that the Anabaptist sectarians had arrived. In many cases they were summarily executed, even without a formal trial. Thus they continued to go out as sheep in the midst of wolves, seeking for those who were willing to amend their lives and live according to the Word of Christ, even though large numbers of their members were imprisoned, tortured, drowned, beheaded, strangled, and burned. The missionary motif in Anabaptism has been ably demonstrated in the Frank S. Brewer Prize Essay by Franklin H. Littell.[25]

The Church Must Exhibit God's Will

In addition to the evangelistic and missionary function of the church, there was also the obligation of Christians corporately to exhibit the will of God for his covenant children. Salvation for the Anabaptists was not a private ticket to heaven. It was much more a calling to live out the precepts of Christ and the New Testament in the power of a faith-union with the Lord Jesus. This does not mean that the Anabaptists were perfectionists in ethics; they made no claim to absolute holiness. On the contrary they spoke much of their need for divine grace, of their personal weakness, and of the perversity of their flesh. When Thomas von Imbroich lay in his prison cell in Cologne in 1558, he wrote to his church a typical Anabaptist epistle:

> Therefore, my brethren, and my dear wife, let us be valiant; for the apostle says, "My strength is made perfect in weakness." . . . Hence I deem it good to be in weakness, (mark) if it be followed by being in reproach, distress, persecution, and fear for Christ's sake. . . .
> Yea, if the Lord should count me worthy to testify with my blood to His name, how greatly would I thank Him. For I hope not only to bear these bonds with patience, but also to die for Christ's sake that I may finish my course with joy; for I would rather be with the Lord than live again in this abominable wicked world. However, His divine will be done. Amen.
> And if anything should be defective yet in my life, that I may not have been diligent enough (which I confess), may the Lord blot it out and purge it through the fire of His love and mercy in the blood of Jesus Christ . . . Dear brethren, I desire that you will all pray to God for me that He will keep us through Jesus Christ our Lord and Saviour. Amen.[26]

The church fulfills this second aspect of its mission (exhibiting God's will) insofar as the members individually and corporately manifest the fruit of the Spirit and walk in the ethic of love and holiness as taught by Christ. No member was to live in any known sin; the works of the flesh were to be overcome in the power of the Holy Spirit. Christians should also manifest only love to all men, especially to the members of the church. This love was not merely to be a matter of words, but believers were to help each other in any and every need, be it spiritual or material. The practice of mutual aid, in which each member makes his resources available as needed, was a major Anabaptist emphasis. In only one group, the Hutterian Brethren of Austria, was this principle carried so far as to renounce the individual ownership of property—although the charge of "community of goods" was frequently hurled against the Anabaptists because their mutual-aid concept was not rightly understood by either the civil or religious leaders of the day.

State and Church Contrasted

The Anabaptists drew a sharp contrast between the church and the state. They regarded the state as having a merely human head, while the head of the church was Christ. The state included all men, good and evil, while the church was made up of the regenerated, the true believers. The state is entered by the natural birth, while the church is entered (after the age of personal accountability) by conversion and the new birth. The function of the state is to maintain law and order, while that of the church is to evangelize the world and to create a body of Christian disciples who obey the Word of God and thus exhibit his will before men. The state controls by law, while the church is governed by the Word and Spirit of God. The state employs such sanctions as fines, imprisonment, and death (although some of the Anabaptists opposed capital punishment), while the church can but exclude those who turn away from following Christ. The state will end with the return of Christ, while the church has before it an eternity of glory. One of the earliest summaries of this general point of view is in the Swiss Schleitheim Confession of Faith of 1527.[27] So absolutely were these contrasts

taken that not only did the Anabaptists reject the military because they could not take life; they went so far as refuse the
magistracy because they did not wish to deal with people on any
other basis than with the redemptive message of the gospel. They
felt that God did not hand over the sword of Moses (the maintenance of law and order by force) to the church, but to the
state. And they held absolutely to the separation of church and
state.

It does not follow, however, that the Anabaptists were an-
archists. They were not. They did not believe that it was their
calling to administer justice in a sub-Christian society which
requires the sanctions of law and force. Yet they regarded the
state as a divine institution. Christians are duty-bound, they
held, to obey the laws, to pay their taxes, and to render honor
to the civil authorities as "ministers of God" (Romans 13:1-7).
But they held that when the state attempted to stop the teaching
of God's Word it had stepped out of its divinely prescribed
sphere. The state had no right to establish any creed by law, nor
to punish religious dissenters. The magistrates ought to mind
their proper business of rewarding the good and punishing
evildoers.

The Church Must Be Disciplined

The Anabaptists were most unhappy about the lack of discipline in the state churches of their day. They regarded the
presence of any unrepentant sinners in the church as fatal to its
life and witness. (This applied particularly to the Lutherans,
in the judgment of the Anabaptists.) It is not that the Brethren
were perfectionists; it was simply that they felt that the church
needed to maintain a biblical discipline. In 1551 several Anabaptists fled from Lier in Brabant to Ghent in Flanders. There they
were betrayed into the hands of the authorities, who imprisoned
them, and finally burned them to death without strangling. One
of them, a man named Wouter Denijs, made the following
critical remarks before his execution: "Citizens of Ghent, we

suffer not as heretics or Lutherans who hold in one hand a beer mug, and a Testament in the other, thus dishonoring the Word of God and dealing in drunkenness; but we die for the genuine truth."[28] As the fire was about to be kindled the martyrs said to one another, "Let us fight valiantly for this is our last pain. Hereafter we shall rejoice with God in endless joy."[29]

The Anabaptists and the state churchmen both appealed to the parable of the tares in Matthew 13. The state churchmen held that the parable justified the retention of sinners in the church, for the Lord commanded to let the wheat and tares grow together until the harvest. (Yet the state church clergy favored the persecution of the Anabaptists in accordance with the imperial decrees, for did they not go about at night and hold secret meetings in unseemly times and places, often in the forests, seeking to lead from the faith the members of the state churches?) The Anabaptists, however, held that the parable of the wheat and tares supported the principle of toleration. Saints and sinners (specifically religious dissenters!) should be allowed to live together in the world until Christ's return. The church, however, should restrict its membership to converted people who took the Christian life seriously, and who gave evidence of newness of life in Christ.

Some idea of the importance of church discipline in the minds of the Anabaptists may be gained from the fact that on no other topic did Menno Simons write three books; they were *A Kind Admonition on Church Discipline,* 1541; *A Clear Account of Excommunication,* 1550; and *Instruction on Excommunication,* 1558. Over and over he hammers away at the theme: To be a true church calls for biblical discipline. This does not mean a merciless expulsion for a transgression done in weakness and followed at once by penitence. In fact, church discipline begins with brotherly assistance:

"If you see your brother sin," wrote Menno in 1541, "then do not pass him by . . . if his fall be curable, from that moment endeavor to raise him up by gentle admonition and brotherly instruction before you eat, drink, sleep, or do anything else."[30]

Furthermore, discipline shall be tempered with kindness and love, not be harsh and severe. Indeed, it is the very last step when all else has failed. "Wherefore, brethren, understand correctly. No one is excommunicated or expelled by us from the communion of the brethren but those who have already separated and expelled themselves from Christ's communion either by false doctrine or by improper conduct."[31]

All church discipline must proceed according to the Word of God, not according to human laws and standards. In 1550 Menno wrote near the close of his second book on discipline:

> I have written this out of pure love, and in the interest of peace, according to the direction of the holy Word, before my God who shall judge me at the last day. I know, however, that by some I will not earn much thanks, for to some what I have written will be too stringent and others too lenient. I must bear this as I have done these fifteen years. Still I would pray you for the sake of the merits of the precious blood of my Lord Jesus Christ, that if any one should find fault with this my treatise, be it on account of mildness or stringency, not to do so except with the authority of the Word, Spirit, and life of the Lord, and not recklessly and thoughtlessly, lest he make blunders. Whatsoever any person can advance and prove I will gladly hear and obey; but I dare not go higher nor lower, be more stringent or lenient, than the Scriptures and the Holy Spirit teach me; and that out of great fear and anxiety of my conscience lest I once more burden the God-fearing hearts (who now have renounced the commandments of men) with more such commandments. Willfulness and human opinions I roundly hate, and do not want them. I know what tribulation and affliction they have caused me for many years.[32]

But when all necessary safeguards have been set up, the main point still stands for Menno. The church has no choice; discipline must be exercised! Menno wrote in 1558:

> It is evident that the congregation or church cannot continue in the saving doctrine, in an unblamable and pious life, without the proper use of excommunication. For as a city without walls and gates, or a field without trenches and fences, and a house without walls and doors, so is also a

church which has not the true apostolic exclusion or ban. . . . it is the distinguished usage, honor, and prosperity of a sincere church if it with Christian discretion teaches the true apostolic separation, and observes it carefully in solicitous love according to the ordinance of the holy, sacred Scriptures. It is more than evident that if we had not been zealous in this matter these days we would be considered and called by every man the companions of the sect of Münster and all perverted sects. Now, however, thank God for His grace, by the proper use of this means of the sacred ban, it is well known among many thousands of honorable, reasonable persons in different principalities, cities, and countries, that we are innocent of and free from all godless abominations and all perverted sects. . . .[33]

Limitations of Public Discipline

Church discipline does not apply to private transgressions in the life of a true believer when those transgressions are known only to the believer and His Lord:

> If at any time one should in a carnal abomination sin against God in private (from which may His power preserve us all), and should the Spirit of the grace of Christ, which alone works genuine repentance in us, once more take hold of our heart and grant genuine repentance: in this matter we are not so to judge, for it is a matter between a man and his God. For since it is evident that we seek our righteousness and salvation, the remission of our sins, satisfaction, reconciliation, and eternal life, not in or through the ban, but solely in the righteousness, intercession, merits, death, and blood of Christ: therefore, since the two objectives for which the ban is commanded in the Scriptures have no legitimate function in this case (in the first place, because the sin is private and no infection can for that reason be occasioned, and in the second place, because his heart is already touched and his life penitent, and consequently no mortification and regret are necessary) . . . we have no binding key of Christ nor any commandment wherewith to punish him yet more, or . . . shame him before the church.[34]

Finally, in a letter of Menno to a church in Franeker in Friesland, Menno urged:

"Not the weak but the corrupt members are cut off, lest they corrupt the others. . . . I seek to use the ban in a noble, fraternal spirit, in faithful love according to the doctrine of Christ and His apostles. . . ."[35]

No Fellowship with Apostates

The knottiest problem for the Dutch and North German Anabaptists was how far to break spiritual and social fellowship with the excommunicated. For example, how deeply should excommunication cut as between a faithful married partner and the excommunicated mate? Instead of leaving the matter to the good judgment of the individuals involved, the congregations were forever trying to formulate rules on the subject which were difficult to carry out. In vain did Menno plead for tolerance on the subject. He was indeed clear that excommunication was normally to be followed by the "shunning" of the impenitent ex-member (he based this on various passages of the New Testament such as I Corinthians 5:9-11; Romans 16:17; II Thessalonians 3:14), but when it came to married partners Menno's counsel generally was, "Hands off! Do not be too strict in the matter." It may be noted that the Swiss Brethren interpreted these passages as applying primarily to the communion of the Lord's Supper, not to ordinary social intercourse. If only the Dutch "Mennists" could have exercised similar discrimination and tolerance!

V

THE CHRISTIAN LIFE

✠

Repentance Is First

Man's great need is for repentance and faith so that Christ may transform him into his own image and use him in the building of his spiritual Kingdom. This was the conviction of the Anabaptists. This hope of seeing men spiritually renewed drove them all over Europe in an effort to spread the gospel. Indeed, a conference of leaders was held at Augsburg in Swabia on August 20, 1527, and missioners were sent out two by two to many areas of German-speaking Europe. So many of these evangelists were captured and martyred that the conference got the significant name, the Martyrs' Synod. Remarkable conversions nevertheless occurred. One curious explanation of the rapid spread of Anabaptism in the early years of the movement was that the missioners carried little flasks with them, and whoever drank from their flasks was bewitched and charmed into uniting with the church of the "hedgepreachers"! The concept of the necessity of a personal conversion to Christ stood in sharp contrast with the territorial church system which prevailed in those days, and even greater was the contrast with all sacramentarian theories. For the Anabaptists only one road led to Christ and heaven: that was the path of suffering discipleship which began with penitence and contrition.

"My dearly beloved reader," wrote Menno in his book, *The New Birth,* about 1537,

> take heed to the Word of the Lord and learn to know the true God. I warn you faithfully . . . He will not save you nor forgive your sins nor show you his mercy and grace except according to His Word; namely, if you repent and if you be-

lieve, if you are born of Him, if you do what He has commanded and walk as He walks. For if He could save an
unrighteous carnal man without regeneration, faith, and repentance, then He did not teach us the truth. . . . Therefore,
I tell you again that you cannot be reconciled by means of all
the masses, matins, vespers, ceremonies, sacraments, councils,
statutes, and commandments under the whole heavens, which
the popes and their colleges have made from the beginning.
For they are abominations and not reconciliations . . . But
if you wish to be saved, by all means and first of all your
earthly, carnal, ungodly life must be reformed. For it is naught
but true repentance that the Scriptures teach and enjoin
upon us with admonitions, threatenings, reprovings, miracles,
examples, ceremonies, and sacraments. If you do not repent
there is nothing in heaven or on earth that can help you,
for without true repentance we are comforted in vain.[1]

And yet it is also true that repentance is the response of a
sinner to the gracious prompting of God in his soul. It is nothing
which the sinner can initiate himself. He will not of himself turn
to Christ. In discussing the conversion of the malefactor on
the cross (*The True Christian Faith,* c. 1541) Menno writes:

And so . . . take heed. This poor penitent sinner will
rise up against those who have comforted themselves with
him in their sins, and accuse and condemn them before the
face of His Majesty. For they have so often heard the sweet
sound of the harp and the new song (that is, the divine
Word), and have never with joyful gratitude rejoiced in it,
nor ever learned or believed it with open and renewed hearts.
But this man heard it but once and immediately believed.

Ah, dear children, beware, and seek Christ while He may
still be found. And call on Him while He is still near, lest
His anger go forth and the fire of His fierce wrath consume
you. Do you think . . . that you can receive faith, repentance,
sorrow for sin, and the grace of God whenever it suits you?
Oh, no! . . .[2]

But the most important facet of the Anabaptist doctrine of
repentance was its continuous nature. This continuing spiritual
hunger and penitence they called in German, *Bussfertigkeit,* a
rather difficult term to translate with one word. It signified a

spirit of penitence and contrition. The attitude designated by it stands in contrast with a self-satisfied spirit, with being content with one's spiritual condition—if not possessed even of spiritual pride! The term *Bussfertigkeit* runs strongly through the Anabaptist literature. In the great Disputation held at Bern in 1538, a spokesman for the Swiss Brethren gave this testimony:

> [While yet in the state church] We obtained much instruction from the writings of Luther, Zwingli, and others concerning the mass and other papal ceremonies, that they are vain. Yet I realized a great lack, for we were not led into a Christian life, repentance and true Christianity, upon which my mind was bent. I waited and hoped a year or two, since the minister had much to say of amendment of life, giving to the poor, loving one another, and abstaining from evil. But I could not close my eyes to the fact that the doctrine which was preached and which was based on God's word was not carried out. No beginning was made toward true Christian living, for there was no unison in the teaching concerning these things. And although the mass and the images were finally abolished, there was no true repentance, no evidence of Christian love. . . . There was only a superficial change. This gave me occasion to inquire further into these things. Then God sent His messengers, Conrad Grebel and others, with whom I conferred about the fundamental teachings of the Apostles and the Christian life. I found them men who had surrendered themselves by *Bussfertigkeit* to the doctrine of Christ, and with their assistance we founded and established a congregation in which repentance and newness of life in Christ were in evidence.[3]

Justified by Faith

The Anabaptists have often been accused of legalism, of being weak on the doctrine of justification by faith, of having a low view of grace. The fact is that they asserted the New Testament doctrine of salvation by faith alone in the very strongest terms. Ponder this gem from Menno's *Confession of the Distressed Christians,* 1552:

Think not, beloved reader, that we boast of being perfect and without sins. Not at all. As for me I confess that often my prayer is mixed with sin and my righteousness with unrighteousness; for by the grace of God I feel (if I but observe the anointing which is in me) when I compare my weak nature to Christ and His commandment, what kind of flesh I have inherited from Adam. If God should judge us according to our deserts and not according to His great goodness and mercy, then I confess with the holy David that no man could stand before His judgment. . . . Therefore it should be far from us that we should comfort ourselves with anything but the grace of God through Christ Jesus. For He it is and He alone and none other who has perfectly fulfilled the righteousness required by God. . . . For Christ's sake we are in grace; for His sake we are heard; and for His sake our faults and failings which are committed against our will are remitted. For it is He who stands between His Father and His imperfect children with His perfect righteousness, and with His innocent blood and death, and intercedes for all those who believe on Him. . . .

Notice, my dear reader, that we do not believe nor teach that we are to be saved by our merits and works. . . .[4]

That which appropriates these unmerited blessings from Christ is faith. And faith is no mere opinion of the mind, divorced from character and life. On the contrary, faith is that by which a man lives. What he believes he lives. The Anabaptists had an existential kind of Christianity much like that of the great reformer of the eighteenth century, John Wesley, or like the strangely modern Dane, Søren Kierkegaard (died 1855). In *The True Christian Faith,* Menno explained:

All the truly regenerated and spiritually minded conform in all things to the Word and ordinances of the Lord. Not because they think to merit the atonement of their sins and eternal life. By no means. In this matter they depend upon nothing except the true promise of the merciful Father, given in grace to all believers through the blood and merits of Christ . . . a truly believing Christian is thus minded that he will not do otherwise than that which the Word of the Lord teaches and enjoins . . .[5]

I have read recently that they write that there is but one

good work which saves us, namely faith; and but one sin that will damn us, namely unbelief. I will let this pass without finding fault, for where there is a genuine, true faith there also are all manner of genuine, good fruits. On the other hand, where there is unbelief there also are all manner of evil fruits. Therefore salvation is properly ascribed to faith, and damnation to unbelief.[6]

The true evangelical faith which makes the heart upright and pious before God moves, changes, urges, and constrains a man so that he will always hate the evil and gladly do the things which are right and good. . . . It is unnecessary to admonish or warn those who sincerely believe that the wages of sin is death, that drunkards, liars, fornicators, adulterers, the avaricious, idolators, those who despise God, hate, shed blood, swear falsely, steal, etc., shall not inherit the kingdom of Christ. . . . For their faith which is sealed unto them by the Spirit through the Word teaches them that the end thereof is death.[7]

Menno placed on the title page of each of his books, "For no other foundation can anyone lay than that which is laid, which is Jesus Christ."

Anabaptist Emphases

In 1572 Jan Wouters van Kuijck was living in Dordrecht in Holland, moving about frequently so as not to be apprehended by the authorities. Somehow the bailiff learned where he was residing and came with his beadles to capture Jan. He met them at the door and when they asked, "Does Jan van Kuijck live here?", he replied in a loud voice that he was the man. (He spoke loudly to warn his wife to flee, which she promptly did successfully.) He was tortured and scourged in the prison and finally burned at the stake on March 28, 1572. He wrote a dozen letters which have been preserved. To his only daughter he wrote a description of those of true faith which is an excellent summary of the emphases of the Anabaptists of the sixteenth century on the necessity of each believer taking up his cross:

[When you come to years of understanding] Diligently search . . . the holy Scriptures and you will find that we must follow Christ Jesus and obey Him unto the end; and you will also truly find the little flock who follow Christ. And this is the sign: they lead a penitent life; they avoid that which is evil, and delight in doing what is good; they hunger and thirst after righteousness; they are not conformed to the world; they crucify their sinful flesh more and more every day, to die unto sin which wars in their members; they strive and seek after that which is honest and of good report; they do evil to no one; they pray for their enemies; they do not resist their enemies; their words are yea that is yea, and nay that is nay; their word is their seal; they are sorry that they do not constantly live more holily, for which reason they often sigh and weep. Let not this however be the only sign by which you may know who follows Christ; but [they are] also these, namely who bear the cross of Christ, for He says: "If any man will come after me, let him deny himself, and take up his cross daily, and follow me."[8]

Jan also submitted a letter to the authorities, the bailiff, the burgomasters, the aldermen, and the council of the city of Dordrecht. The following brief extracts illustrate the thinking of a typical Anabaptist:

I, Jan Wouters, your prisoner, not for any crime but for the sake of my faith, which is nevertheless right before my God, wish you, you ministers of God, that He would grant you all a prosperous, peaceful, healthy, long life; and understanding [of how] rightly to use your office in punishing the evil [that is, evildoers] and protecting the good. . . .

I confess that I was a zealous papist in my youth, which I heartily regret . . . Afterwards God opened my blind eyes . . . And He revealed to and gave me, poor sinful man, the faith of the truth by which we are saved. . . . This faith and the inward baptism constrained me to the obedience of His Word to fulfill His righteousness. Hence I confess that I was baptized upon my faith . . . according to the command of Christ, renouncing the devil, the world, the pope, and his adherents.

I confess Christ Jesus alone as the way, the truth, and the life. And there is none other name given to men whereby we can be saved, except through Christ alone. I further confess that it is certain that the customs of the priests and of all the "shaved" are the broad way to damnation. . . .

I also confess that I have attended the assembly of the believers so often that I cannot count it. . . . I confess that I am a sinful man and need every day to confess my sins before my God and daily to die unto sin more and more . . .

I also confess that I did not marry my wife secretly that no one should see it, but before the church of God; for marriage is honorable . . . O my God, count it not sin to him who took me away, for it is a bitter cup to me to part from wife and child because we love one another so much. . . .

Finally, deal mercifully with me, innocent one, and think that I too am a man, for hereafter he "shall have judgment without mercy that hath shewed no mercy." . . . I confess one Lord, one faith, one God, one Father of all, who is above all, and in all believers. I believe only what the holy Scriptures say, and not what men say. Farewell. Written in my bonds.[9]

Before Jan was taken to the place of execution, his mouth was gagged so that he could not speak to the people who would assemble for his burning. Somehow he managed to get rid of the gag. A fellow believer pressed close to him on the way to the stake and said, "Strive valiantly, dear Brother, you will suffer no more hereafter." Jan pulled open his shirt and showed him his body bloody from the scourging as he replied, "I already bear in my body the marks of the Lord Jesus."

Just before the fire was kindled he looked over the crowd and cried, "Adieu and farewell, my dear brethren and sisters, I will herewith commend you to the Lord, to the Lord who shed His blood for us." Then as the fire was about to initiate his slow death he prayed, "O God, who art my strength, I commend my spirit into Thy hands." Thus perished another of several thousand free-church martyrs.

Faithful Discipleship to the Prince of Peace

The Brethren thought of the essence of the Christian life as discipleship to Christ. This meant walking as he walked, not in human strength but by the power of the Holy Spirit. Although human weakness and infirmity stay with every believer, no matter how mature in faith and experience, yet the Brethren believed that Christ's redemption actually did break the power of sin in the believer. Temptations to hatred, lust, avarice, vengeance, and the like still come to Christians, but in Christ they are able to come off victorious.

The most striking Anabaptist deviation from the traditional Christian ethic was the espousal of the doctrine of absolute love and nonresistance. This was no philosophical pacifism, but it was an effort to walk in love as Christ walked. The Anabaptists sought such an infilling of divine love that they could love even their persecutors. Many martyrs gave evidence of just such love as they forgave their tormentors, the judges who sentenced them, and the executioners who destroyed them. They were willing to die for Jesus, they were prepared to suffer in any way God permitted, but they did not feel free to hate or harm anyone. It was this doctrine of nonresistance which they based squarely on the explicit teaching of Christ and his Apostles which made them refuse both the magistracy and the military. They were ready to die but not to kill.

In his *Brief and Clear Confession,* 1544, Menno wrote:

> Behold, beloved friends and brethren, by these and other Scriptures we are taught and warned not to take up the literal sword nor ever to give our consent thereto (except the ordinary sword of the magistrate when it must be used) but to take up the two-edged, powerful, sharp sword of the Spirit which goes forth from the mouth of God, namely the Word of God.[10]

And in his *Reply to False Accusations* of 1552 Menno added:

> All Christians are commanded to love their enemies, to do good unto those who abuse and persecute them, to give the mantle when the cloak is taken, the other cheek when one is struck. . . .
> O beloved reader, our weapons are not swords and spears, but patience, silence, and hope, and the Word of God. . . .

True Christians do not know vengeance, no matter how they are mistreated. . . . They do not cry, Vengeance, vengeance, as does the world; but with Christ they supplicate and pray, "Father, forgive them; for they know not what they do."[11]

In the year 1569, a pious brother named Dirk Willems of Asperen in Holland learned that officers were about to arrest him in his home. He fled out the back door with the officers in pursuit. Coming to a frozen dyke he ventured to flee across on the ice, which he managed to do. But the officer who attempted to follow him broke through and was about to perish in the icy water. Thereupon Dirk, in true compassion, turned back and assisted the officer to safety. Dirk's only reward was to be burned at the stake as an Anabaptist heretic. The Catholic judges passed sentence on him May 16, 1569. On the day of his burning at the stake such a strong wind blew that he suffered a very slow death. He was heard to cry out over seventy times, "O my Lord; O my God." Finally, the bailiff, who was on horseback, wheeled his horse around and shouted, "Dispatch the man with a quick death." The account does not report in what manner his misery was terminated.

A century and a half ago there lived in Philadelphia a prominent leader in Colonial America named Dr. Benjamin Rush (1745-1813). He was a physician, a member of the Continental Congress, and a signer of the Declaration of Independence. He seems to have given some thought to the matter of war and bloodshed. He ventured this optimistic comment on such groups as the Mennonites and the German Baptists (now known as the Church of the Brethren) : "Perhaps those German sects of Christians who refuse to bear arms for the shedding of human blood may be preserved by divine Providence as the center of a circle which shall gradually embrace all nations of the earth in a perpetual treaty of friendship and peace." His prophecy certainly shows little sign of ever being fulfilled. And yet should not this hope be the prayer of all Christendom? Ought not men learn to dwell together in peace and harmony, with young people free to establish Christian homes, and with the whole church unhindered in its great commission to make disciples of all the nations? Ought we not all cry to the Father that through Jesus Christ the day might soon come when people "shall beat their swords into plowshares . . . neither shall they learn war any more" (Isaiah 2:4).

VI

EVEN UNTO DEATH

✠

The sixteenth-century chronicler, Sebastian Franck, wrote in 1531 concerning the Swiss Brethren in Switzerland and South Germany:

> The Anabaptists spread so rapidly that their teaching soon covered, as it were, the land. They soon gained a large following and baptized many thousands, drawing to themselves many sincere souls who had a zeal for God. For they taught nothing but love, faith, and the cross. They showed themselves humble, patient under much suffering; they brake bread with one another as an evidence of unity and love. They helped each other faithfully, called each other brother, etc. They increased so rapidly that the world feared an uprising by them, though I have learned that this fear had no justification whatsoever. They were persecuted with great tyranny, being imprisoned, branded, tortured, and executed by fire, water, and sword. In a few years very many were put to death. Some have estimated the number of those who were killed to be far above two thousand. They died as martyrs, patiently, and humbly endured all persecution.

This, of course, was written before the Anabaptist movement of the Netherlands was formally established. In the Netherlands another two thousand five hundred martyrs were destined to die for their Anabaptist "heresy."

A Man of God Burned

One of the most outstanding Anabaptists in terms of personality, scholarship, and general ability was Balthasar Hübmaier. Born at Friedberg near Augsburg he secured his baccalaureate degree there in 1510. One of his favorite professors was Johann

Eck (Luther's Catholic opponent who wrote a five-volume critique of Luther and Lutheranism). When Eck transferred to Ingolstadt, Hübmaier followed him and earned not only the licentiate in theology but also a doctor of theology degree. Hübmaier was at that time a Catholic priest, and a man of great ability as a speaker. Gradually he turned toward the evangelical faith of Zwingli. He took various steps which gave evidence of his weakening in Roman doctrine: he began to conduct his services in German rather than Latin; he opposed the use of images in the church; he married Elizabeth Hügeline. He was forced to move about to avoid arrest. In 1523 he and Zwingli agreed on the desirability of baptizing believing converts rather than infants. But the opposition which Zwingli encountered in Grebel, Manz, and Reublin led him in the end to take a vigorous stand in favor of infant baptism. When Zwingli wrote his booklet on infant baptism, Hübmaier replied with one of the ablest treatises on believer's baptism ever written, *Vom christlichen Tauf der Gläubigen* (Concerning the Christian Baptism of Believers). In 1526, after experiencing considerable difficulty in Zurich for a time, Hübmaier fled to Moravia in Austrian territory, where it is reported that there were soon 12,000 Anabaptists, many of them from various parts of South Germany. Hübmaier was a firm advocate of believer's baptism, and therefore an Anabaptist. But on one point he differed with the Swiss Brethren: he did not hold to the doctrine of nonresistance. His followers were therefore called *Schwertler* from the German word for sword.

After accomplishing a heroic work as reformer and writer, Hübmaier was arrested and imprisoned in 1527. He made strenuous efforts to avoid the stake, but in vain. On March 10, 1528, at Vienna he was led forth to be executed. When he arrived at the spot he cried out in Swiss German, "O my gracious God, grant me grace in my great suffering!" He then requested the crowd to forgive him if they had anything against him, and he in turn forgave his enemies. As the fire rose he exclaimed, "O my heavenly Father! O my gracious God!" When his hair and beard began to burn he cried, "O Jesus!" Soon he was dead. The spectators thought that during his suffering his face showed more joy than pain. Thus a noble knight of Christ witnessed to the truth. Hübmaier's motto was, "Divine truth is immortal." Present-day Baptists agree with the truth as Hübmaier taught it. Could he have seen the millions of believers who, four centuries after his martyrdom, joyfully hold to the convictions for which he died, how much greater his joy would have been!

A Cloud of Witnesses

The Zurich congregation of the *Täufer* was no sooner organized than persecution began. The leaders especially were imprisoned for varying lengths of terms, only to be brought forth to execution. It is impossible to make anything like a complete list of early Swiss Brethren martyrs, for few records were kept. Among those known to have been put to death for their "heresy" were: George Blaurock, Eberli Bolt, Wolfgang Brandhuber, Hans Brötli, Offrus Griessinger, Thomas Herman, Jakob Huter, Jerome Käls, Johannes Krüsi, Eitelhans Langenmantel, Hans Ludi, Michael Sattler, Leonard Schiemer, Hans Schlaffer, Hans Leopold Schneider, Leonard Seiler, Wolfgang Uliman, and George Zaunring. Langenmantel's case is fairly typical.

Eitelhans Langenmantel sprang from a patrician family of Augsburg; his own father had served fourteen terms as mayor of the city and was also captain of the Swabian League for many years. In 1527 Langenmantel accepted baptism and was received into the Anabaptist congregation of the city. Before the year was out he was arrested for his "heresy." Because of his prominent connections he got off lightly; he was briefly imprisoned and banished. He seems to have made some sort of promise to withdraw from the Anabaptists and to recognize infant baptism again. But actually he did not in the end abandon his basic convictions. On April 24, 1528, he was seized by a man named Diebold von Stein, captain of the Swabian League, and put in chains. A few weeks later he was beheaded—sitting in his chair for the execution because of the pain of gout! Langenmantel was the author of a number of booklets, including an exposition of the Lord's Prayer, and a treatise on the Lord's Supper, *Von Nachtmahl des Herren.* His execution took place on May 11, 1528, two months and a day after Hübmaier's.

By the end of 1531, the number of Anabaptist martyrs in the Tirol and Gorizia was estimated to have reached a total of one thousand. In the Tirolese town of Kitzbühl alone, sixty-eight were executed in one year.

Legal Procedures Employed

There was a remarkable similarity in dealing with the Anabaptists regardless of time and place. Whether one examines the great tome, *The Martyrs Mirror* of 1660, or the 1957 German monograph of Dr. Horst W. Schraepler, *The Juridical Treatment of the Anabaptists,* the picture is the same. If passing laws and issuing edicts could have stopped the movement, it surely would have come to an end. No less than 222 known mandates were issued against the Anabaptists between 1525 and 1761. Fifty-nine of them appeared within the first five years of the movement. They appeared in Zurich, Saxony, St. Gall, Grisons, Basel, Bamberg, Strasbourg, Augsburg, Salzburg, Upper Austria, Bavaria, Baden, Württemberg, Brandenburg, Mainz, the Palatinate; wherever there were Anabaptists the rulers kept issuing new mandates or renewed older ones. These mandates threatened (1) expulsion from the city or land, (2) fines, (3) corporal punishment, (4) capital punishment, (5) confiscation of property, (6) execution without trial, (7) burning at the stake for those not recanting, and (8) beheading for those who do recant. The Imperial Diet of Spires, 1529, representing both Catholic and evangelical rulers, had ordered that every Anabaptist and rebaptized person of either sex should be put to death by fire, sword, or in some other way. This decree seems to have been followed all over the Holy Roman Empire, with two notable exceptions: the city of Strasbourg never executed a single Anabaptist (it imprisoned and banished them), and the Landgrave of Hesse, Philip I, never put any Anabaptists to death. The decision of Philip of Hesse not to kill the Anabaptists caused one Anabaptist to die in jail after a harrowing seventeen years of imprisonment. The man's name was Fritz Erbe. He was arrested in the county of Hausbreitenbach, which was under the joint supervision of Saxony and Hesse. The Elector of Saxony felt strongly that it was imperative to execute Erbe in conformity with the Edict of Spires, while Philip was just as firm that he would not shed blood for matters of faith. He supported his position by referring to the views of the church fathers, Augustine and Chrysostom. Erbe, for part of his imprisonment, was in a tower on the city wall at Eisenach. Some of his Anabaptist brethren used to gather in the dead of night and quietly converse with him. In November 1535, two of these visitors were apprehended. Since this was in Saxon territory Philip had no jurisdiction over their fate. Spires prevailed. They were executed in November 1537.

A Catholic sentence of 1571 at Amsterdam will illustrate the common attitude toward the Anabaptists:

Sentence of Death of Anneken Heyndricks, Surnamed De Vlaster

Whereas, Anna Heyndricks daughter, *alias,* Anna de Vlaster, formerly [a] citizeness of this city, at present a prisoner here, unmindful of her soul's salvation, and the obedience which she owed to our mother, the holy church, and to his royal majesty, as her natural lord and prince, rejecting the ordinances of the holy church, has neither been to confession, nor to the holy, worthy sacrament, for six or seven years since, [but has dared] to go into the assembly of the reprobated sect of the Mennonists, or Anabaptists, and has also held conventicles or meetings at her house; and has further, about three years ago, forsaking and renouncing the baptism received in her infancy from the holy church, been rebaptized, and then received the breaking of bread according to the manner of the Mennonist sect, and was also married to her present husband in Mennonist manner, by night, in a country house; and though she, the prisoner, has, by my lords of the court, as well as by divers ecclesiastical persons, been urged and repeatedly admonished, to leave the afore-mentioned reprobated sect, she nevertheless refuses to do it, persisting in her obstinacy and stubbornness, so that she, the prisoner, according to what has been mentioned, has committed crime against divine and human majesty, as by said sect disturbing the common peace and welfare of the land, according to the import of the decrees of his majesty, existing in regard to this; which misdemeanors, for an example unto others, ought not to go unpunished; therefore, my lord of the court, having heard the demand of my lord the bailiff, seen the confession of the prisoner, and having had regard to her obstinacy and stubbornness, have condemned her, and condemn her by these presents, to be, according to the decrees of his royal majesty, executed with fire, and declare all her property confiscated for the benefit of his majesty aforesaid. Done in court, on the 10th of November, in the year 1571, in presence of the judges, by the advice of all the burgomasters, in my knowledge, as secretary, and as was subscribed: W. Pieterss.[1]

A Martyr Epistle

The martyrs frequently found it possible to smuggle letters from prison to their relatives and fellow believers. Here is a sample letter:

Know, my beloved wife, that yesterday about three o'clock I had written you a letter, which I now send you. I could not send it then, for soon afterwards the margrave came here to torture us; hence I was not able to send the letter, for then all four of us were one after another severely tortured, so that we have now but little inclination to write; however, we cannot forbear; we must write to you.

Cornelis the shoemaker was the first; then came Hans Symons, with whom also the captain went down into the torture chamber. Then thought I: "We shall have a hard time of it; to satisfy him." My turn came next—you may think how I felt. When I came to the rack, where were the lords, the order was: "Strip yourself, or tell where you live." I looked distressed, as may be imagined. I then said: "Will you ask me nothing further then?" They were silent.

Then thought I: "I see well enough what it means, it would not exempt me from the torture," hence I undressed, and fully resigned myself to the Lord, to die. Then they racked me dreadfully, twisting off two cords, I believe, on my thighs and shins; they stretched me out, and poured much water into my body and my nose, and also on my heart. Then they released me, and asked: "Will you not yet tell it?" They entreated me, and again they spoke harshly to me; but I did not open my mouth, so firmly had God closed it.

Then they said: "Go at him again, and this with a vengeance." This they also did, and cried: "Go on, go on, stretch him another foot." Then thought I: "You can only kill me." And thus stretched out, with cords twisted around my head, chin, thighs, and shins, they left me lie, and said: "Tell, tell."

They then talked with one another of my account which J. T. had written, of the linen, which amounted to six hundred and fifty-five pounds; and that it was so much cash and rebate. Then the margrave said: "He understands the French well"; and I lay there in pain. Again I was asked: "Will you not tell it?" I did not open my mouth. Then they said: "Tell us where you live; your wife and children, at all events, are all gone away." In short, I said not a word. "What a dreadful thing," they said. Thus the Lord kept my lips, so that I did not open them; and they released me, when they had long tried to make me speak. . . .

By me, your weak husband, Christian Langedul, in prison at Antwerp, the 12th of August 1567.

I have not fully recovered yet from the torture, as may be imagined; but I trust it is all well; do not grieve too much about it. If J. T. could bring along my account book, I should be glad; I should show him everything, or write it down for him. Bring us something to seal letters with.[2]

Two Lovers Die for Jesus

Some of the cases were especially moving. In 1573 a young Anabaptist and his wife, John and Janneken van Munstdorp by name, were arrested in a meeting of Dutch Anabaptists and imprisoned at Antwerp. From his prison cell Jan addressed a loving letter to his bride of less than a year:

An affectionate greeting to you, my beloved wife, whom I love from the heart and greatly cherish above every other creature, and must now forsake for the truth, for the sake of which we must count all things loss and love Him above all. I hope though men separate us here that the Lord will again join us together in His eternal kingdom where no one will be able to part us and we shall reign forever in the heavenly abode. . . .

Adieu and farewell, my lamb, my love; adieu and farewell to all that fear God; adieu and farewell until the marriage of the Lamb in the New Jerusalem. Be valiant and of good cheer; cast the troubles that assail you upon the Lord and He will not forsake you; cleave to Him and you will not fall. Love God above all; have love and truth; love your salvation and keep your promises to the Lord.

John was executed first, by burning at the stake. Janneken was spared to bear her child. Soon after his martyrdom she gave birth to a little daughter to whom she gave her own name. Before her death, also at the stake, Janneken wrote a moving letter to her little child. The letter set forth the familiar sixteenth-century Anabaptist belief in the cross of the Christian disciple. After reporting how her parents had died, and entreating her not to be ashamed of her executed parents, she continued her letter thus:

Hence, my young lamb for whose sake I still have and have had great sorrow, seek when you have attained your understanding this narrow way though there is sometimes much danger in it according to the flesh, as we may see and read if we diligently examine and read the Scriptures, that much is said concerning the cross of Christ. And there are many in this world who are enemies of the cross, who seek to be free from it among the world and to escape it. But, my dear child if we would with Christ seek and inherit salvation we must also help bear His cross. And this is the cross which He would have us bear: to follow His footsteps and to help bear His reproach, for Christ Himself says: "Ye shall be persecuted, killed, and dispersed for my name's sake." Yea, He Himself went before us in this way of reproach, and left us an example that we should follow His steps; for, for His sake all must be forsaken, father, mother, sister, brother, husband, child, yea, one's own life. . . .

And, my dear child, this is my request of you since you are still very little and young—I wrote this when you were but one month old—as I am soon now to offer up my sacrifice by the help of the Lord I leave you this: "That you fulfill my request, always uniting with them that fear God; and do not regard the pomp and boasting of the world, nor the great multitude whose way leads to the abyss of hell, but look at the little flock of Israelites who have no freedom anywhere and must always flee from one land to the other as Abraham did, that you may hereafter obtain your fatherland. For if you seek your salvation it is easy to perceive which is the way that leads to life, or the way that leads into hell. . . ."

I leave you here. Oh, that it had pleased the Lord that I might have brought you up! I should so gladly have done my best with respect to it; but it seems that it is not the Lord's will. And though it had not come thus, and I had remained with you for a time, the Lord could still take me from you; and then, too, you should have to be without me— even as it has now gone with your father and myself: that we could live together but so short a time when we were so well joined; since the Lord had so well mated us that we would not have forsaken each other for the whole world. And yet we had to leave each other for the Lord's sake. So I must also leave you here, my dearest lamb; the Lord that created and made you now takes me from you: it is His holy will. I must now pass through this narrow way which the prophets and martyrs of Christ passed through and many thousands who put off the mortal clothing, who died here for Christ, and now they wait under the altar till their number shall be fulfilled, of which number your dear father is one. And I am now on the point of following him. . . .

I herewith commend you to the Lord and to the comforting Word of His grace, and bid you adieu once more. I hope to wait for you; follow me, my dearest child.

Once more adieu, my dearest upon earth; adieu and nothing more; adieu, follow me; adieu and farewell . . .[3]

Survival and Renewal

The results of the program to crush the Anabaptist movement were generally successful except in three areas: (1) In Bern, Switzerland, a weak minority managed to survive until full religious freedom came in 1874; (2) in Austrian Moravia the

Hutterian Brethren, who held to "community of goods," living communally, held out until their removal to Russia in the latter eighteenth century (where they remained for a hundred years and then settled near what is now Marion, South Dakota); (3) in Holland the followers of Obbe and Dirk Philips, and later of Menno Simons and others, survived a bloody seventy-five years, until William of Orange brought toleration to that land. The Dutch Mennonites became rich and prosperous in the eighteenth century but lost their earlier spiritual dynamic, and their membership fell sharply (from 160,000 in 1700 to 27,000 in 1809). But all over Europe the Anabaptists were otherwise largely annihilated. The present-day Mennonites of South Germany are descendants of the Swiss Brethren. (The Swiss historically called themselves *Taufgesinnten*, i.e., Baptism-minded.) The Anabaptists of the Rhineland, North Germany, and Danzig were of Dutch Anabaptist background. (The Dutch Anabaptists call themselves *Doopsgezinden*, the exact equivalent of the Swiss *Taufgesinnten*.) In the United States most of the Mennonites east of the Mississippi are of Swiss background, while those of the prairie states—Minnesota, the Dakotas, Nebraska, Kansas— are half Swiss and half Dutch by ancestry. The baptized Mennonites of North America total a scant quarter million, and those in Europe and Russia number about a hundred thousand.

In the early seventeenth century Anabaptism revived in England under the influence of such men of God as John Smyth and Thomas Helwys. Out of this movement came the great Baptist Church of modern times, with twenty million members in the United States alone. Baptists do not follow their Anabaptist forbears in every detail, but they are crystal clear on such major biblical truths as the free church, believer's baptism, liberty of conscience, and a brotherhood type of church.

An Ancient Chronicler's Summary

One of the finest accounts of the persecution of the Anabaptists is that given by one of the chroniclers of the Hutterian Brethren, excerpts of which follow:

. . . Many were dealt with in wonderful ways, rare and unheard-of, often by day and by night, with great craftiness and roguery; also with many sweet and smooth words, by monks and priests, by doctors of theology, with much false teaching and testimony, with many threats and menaces, with insults and abuse, yea, with lies and dreadful slanders, but they did not [succeed in making] them despondent.

As some of them lay in grievous imprisonment they sang hymns of praise to God, as those who are in great joy. Some did likewise as they were being led out to death and the place of execution; as those going to meet the bridegroom at a wedding they sang out joyfully with uplifted voice that rang out loudly. Many maidens, when they were to go to the place of execution, adorned themselves, dressing up and making themselves attractive, with the delight of a day of rejoicing, as those who have experienced a heavenly joy—yea, as those who are to pass through the gates of everlasting joy. Others stepped up with a smile on their lips, praising God that they were accounted worthy of dying the death of sincere and Christian heroes, and would not have wished to die [a natural death] in bed. Others exhorted the spectators most earnestly to repentance and amendment of life. Others were cut short and had not received water baptism [but] hastened nevertheless to the baptism of blood, to be baptized therewith for the sake of God's truth, on their living faith— some whom we could name, but of that there is no need. Yea, many who never came to the congregation, and never saw it, but who had merely heard the truth and understood and believed it, remained steadfast therein, so that they were taken away. They did not allow themselves to be terrified or moved by fire, water, sword, or executioner. No human being and nothing on earth could take anything from their hearts, such zealous lovers of God were they. The fire of God burned within them. They preferred to die the bitterest death, yea ten deaths, rather than forsake the truth they had come to know. They would accept nothing as the price of their faith in Christ, no glory, no principality, no kingdom, yea not all the pleasure and wealth of the world, for they had a foundation and an assurance in their faith.

From the shedding of this innocent blood arose Christians everywhere, and fellow believers in all those places here and there; it was not without fruit. Many were moved thereby to serious thought, and to order their life, their thinking and striving, in preparation for the future. Finally the exe-

cutions were carried on in many places at night, as in the
county of the Tirol. The executions were done in secret and
and at night, so that not many people would see, hear, or
know of them. They were also done elsewhere than at the
customary places of execution because they killed them ille-
gally, condemning the innocent, sometimes murderously without a sentence.

In some places they filled the prisons and jails with them,
as did the Count Palatine on the Rhine, supposing that they
could dampen and extinguish the fire of God. But in prison
they sang and were joyful. Nothing was of any avail. The
enemies outside, who thought that the prisoners in jail should
be fearful, themselves became much more afraid, and did not
know what to do with them. For they became aware, for the
most part, of their innocence. Many lay in jails and prisons,
some for a shorter and some for a longer time, some for many
years. They endured all sorts of torture and pain. Some had
holes burned through their cheeks after which they were
released. A portion of them got out in an upright manner
through the help of God, some through wonderful and special
means and providences of God, and thereafter persevered in
the faith unwaveringly until God took them.

Everywhere much slander and evil was spoken of them,
that they had goats-feet and ox-hoofs, and that when they
gave people to drink out of a little flask, thereafter they had
to do like they. They also lied about them that they had
their wives in common . . . that they slew and ate their
children. . . .

But when our Lord Jesus Christ will come in flaming fire,
with many thousands of angels, to hold the judgment on
his great Day, everything will again come forth. The earth
will bring out the blood which it drank in, and will not hide
its slain. The sea shall give up its dead which are therein,
which have been burned to dust and ashes, and they shall
arise and come forth. That will be a different judgment from
that which the world now holds. . . .

But the holy martyrs of God who are now in every distress
will enter upon and receive a beautiful crown, a glorious
kingdom, a great joy, a heavenly rest, an eternal life, an
everlasting salvation, an eternal and immeasurably weighty
and excellent glory. The suffering of this present time is
not worthy of that glory which no eye has seen, nor ear heard,
nor has it entered into any human heart, nor is any tongue

so eloquent as to be able to speak what God has prepared for those who love Him. This blessedness and glory shall have no temporal place and no end, but shall endure from eternity to eternity for ever and ever.[4]

Soli Deo Gloria!

NOTES AND ACKNOWLEDGMENTS

NOTES AND
ACKNOWLEDGMENTS

✠

I. THE SWISS CRADLE OF ANABAPTISM

1. Harold S. Bender, *Conrad Grebel*. Goshen, Indiana: The Mennonite Historical Society, 1950.
2. Leonhard von Muralt and Walter Schmid, *Quellen zur Geschichte der Täufer in der Schweiz*. Zurich: S. Hirzel Verlag, 1952.
3. Harold S. Bender, editor, *The Mennonite Encyclopedia*, Vol. III, p. 473. Scottdale, Pennsylvania: The Mennonite Publishing House, 1957.
4. Guy F. Hershberger, editor, *The Recovery of the Anabaptist Vision*, pp. 57-58. Scottdale, Pennsylvania: Herald Press, 1957.

II. ANABAPTISTS IN THE NETHERLANDS

1. *The Library of Christian Classics*, Volume XXV: *Spiritual and Anabaptist Writers*, edited by George Huntston Williams and Angel M. Mergal. Philadelphia: The Westminster Press, 1957.
2. Published at Elkhart, Indiana, by the Mennonite Publishing Co.
3. See *The Complete Writings of Menno Simons*. Scottdale, Pennsylvania: Herald Press, 1956. In some of the quotations from this book punctuation has been altered.
4. *Ibid.*, p. 204.
5. *Ibid.*, p. 300. (*Oorsake von M. S. leeren en schrijven* [Why Menno Simons Teaches and Writes], 1539.)
6. *Ibid.*, p. 310.
7. *Ibid.*, p. 339.
8. *Ibid.*, p. 484.
9. *Ibid.*, p. 139.
10. *Ibid.*, pp. 396-397.
11. *Ibid.*, p. 93.
12. *Ibid.*, p. 1053.
13. *Ibid.*, pp. 333-334.
14. *Ibid.*, p. 674.
15. *Ibid.*, pp. 599-600.
16. *Ibid.*, p. 539.
17. *Ibid.*, p. 634.
18. *Complete Works of Menno Simons*, Vol. II, p. 451. Elkhart, Indiana: John F. Funk & Brother, 1871.

III. ANABAPTISTS AND THE BIBLE

1. Thieleman J. van Braght, *The Bloody Theater or Martyrs Mirror,* pp. 468-471. Scottdale, Pennsylvania: Mennonite Publishing House, third English edition, 1951. In some quotations from this book punctuation has been altered.
2. *Ibid.,* p. 493.
3. *Ibid.,* pp. 591-611.
4. *Complete Writings,* p. 417.
5. *Martyrs Mirror,* p. 31.
6. D. Philips, *Enchiridion,* pp. 388-389. In some quotations from this book punctuation has been altered.
7. *Ibid.,* pp. 260-261.
8. *Ibid.,* p. 323.
9. *Complete Writings,* p. 217.
10. *Ibid.,* p. 220.
11. *Ibid.,* p. 343.

IV. THE CHURCH AND THE SACRAMENTS

1. *Complete Writings,* p. 300.
2. *Ibid.,* pp. 284-285.
3. *Martyrs Mirror,* pp. 492-493.
4. *Complete Writings,* pp. 138-139.
5. *Ibid.,* p. 139.
6. *Martyrs Mirror,* p. 367.
7. *Ibid.,* p. 370.
8. *Complete Writings,* pp. 280-281.
9. *Martyrs Mirror,* p. 482.
10. *Complete Writings,* p. 153.
11. *Ibid.,* p. 302.
12. *Ibid.,* p. 382.
13. *Ibid.,* p. 232.
14. *Ibid.,* p. 516.
15. *Ibid.,* p. 333.
16. *Ibid.,* p. 105.
17. *Ibid.,* p. 189.
18. *Ibid.,* p. 287.
19. *Ibid.,* p. 362.
20. *Ibid.,* pp. 502-503.
21. *Ibid.,* pp. 962-963.
22. *Ibid.,* pp. 126, 204.
23. The mandate of Emperor Charles V of the Holy Roman Empire, dated January 4, 1528, threatened the Anabaptists with the death penalty. The imperial law against the Anabaptists dated April 23, 1529, and which originated in the Diet of Spires, prescribed death for all Anabaptists without trial, by "fire, sword, or the like." Only those who recanted and begged for mercy were to be spared. (This exception did not apply to Anabaptist preachers. The ordained Anabaptists were to be "ruthlessly" executed.)

24. *Complete Writings*, p. 202.
25. Franklin H. Littell, *The Anabaptist View of the Church*. Second edition, Boston: Starr King Press, 1958.
26. *Martyrs Mirror*, p. 579.
27. The Schleitheim Confession of Faith is printed in J. C. Wenger, *Glimpses of Mennonite History and Doctrine*, pp. 206-213. Scottdale, Pennsylvania: Herald Press, third edition, 1959.
28. *Martyrs Mirror*, p. 503.
29. *Ibid.*
30. *Complete Writings*, pp. 411-412.
31. *Ibid.*, p. 413.
32. *Ibid.*, p. 484.
33. *Ibid.*, p. 962.
34. *Ibid.*, p. 979.
35. *Ibid.*, p. 1044.

V. THE CHRISTIAN LIFE

1. *Complete Writings*, p. 92.
2. *Ibid.*, p. 373.
3. *The Mennonite Quarterly Review*, Vol. 4, October 1931, p. 249.
4. *Complete Writings*, p. 506.
5. *Ibid.*, pp. 396-397.
6. *Ibid.*, p. 399.
7. *Ibid.*, p. 337.
8. *Martyrs Mirror*, p. 915.
9. *Ibid.*, pp. 925-926.
10. *Complete Writings*, pp. 423-424.
11. *Ibid.*, p. 555.

VI. EVEN UNTO DEATH

1. *Martyrs Mirror*, p. 874.
2. *Ibid.*, pp. 705-706.
3. *Ibid.*, pp. 984-987.
4. Rudolph Wolkan, *Geschicht-Buch der Hutterischen Brüder*, pp. 186-189. Macleod, Alta., Canada. 1923. A. J. F. Zieglschmid, *Die älteste Chronik der Hutterischen Brüder* (privately printed, 1943), pp. 237-241. Translated from the German.

BIBLIOGRAPHY

BIBLIOGRAPHY

BIBLIOGRAPHY

✠

Ausbund, das ist: Etliche schöne Christliche Lieder, Wie sie in dem Gefängnis zu Passau . . . von den Schweizer-Brüdern . . . gedichtet worden [Europe, 1564]. Verlag von den Amischen Gemeinden in Lancaster County, Pa., 1935.

Bender, Harold S. *Conrad Grebel*. Goshen, Indiana: The Mennonite Historical Society, 1950.

Bender, Harold S. "The Mennonite Conception of the Church," *The Mennonite Quarterly Review*. Goshen, Indiana, April, 1945, pp. 90-100.

Bender, Harold S. "The Pacifism of the Sixteenth Century Anabaptists," *Church History*. June, 1955, pp. 119-131.

Bender, Harold S. "The Anabaptist Vision," in Guy F. Hershberger, ed., *The Recovery of the Anabaptist Vision*. Scottdale, Pennsylvania: Herald Press, 1957, pp. 29-54.

Bender, Harold S., editor. *The Mennonite Encyclopedia*. Scottdale, Pennsylvania: Mennonite Publishing House, 1955-1959.

Bender, Harold S. "Die Zwickauer Propheten," *Theologische Zeitschrift*. Juli/August 1952, pp. 262-278.

Blanke, Fritz. *Brüder in Christo: Die Geschichte der ältesten Täufergemeinde*. Zollikon, 1525, Zurich, 1955.

Correll, Ernst. *Das schweizerische Täufermennonitentum*. Tübingen, 1925.

Fosdick, Harry Emerson. *Great Voices of the Reformation*. New York: Random House, 1952.

[Geiser, Samuel, *et al.*]. *Die Taufgesinnten Gemeinden*. Karlsruhe, Baden, 1931.

Gratz, Delbert L. *Bernese Anabaptists and their American Descendants. Studies in Anabaptist and Mennonite History*. Scottdale, Pennsylvania: Herald Press, 1953.

Händiges, Emil. *Die Lehre der Mennoniten in Geschichte und Gegenwart*. Eppstein und Ludwigshaven am Rhein, ca. 1921.

Hege, Christian. *Die Täufer in der Kurpfalz*. Frankfurt am Main, 1908.

Hershberger, Guy F. *The Recovery of the Anabaptist Vision*. Scottdale, Pennsylvania: Herald Press, 1957. A sixtieth anniversary tribute to Harold S. Bender, with essays by Professors Bainton, Correll, Fretz, Kreider, Littell, Payne, van der Zijpp, and others.

Hershberger, Guy F. *War, Peace, and Nonresistance*. Scottdale, Pennsylvania: Herald Press, 1953.

Hershberger, Guy F. *The Way of the Cross in Human Relations*. Scottdale, Pennsylvania: Herald Press, 1958.

Hillerbrand, Hans. "An Early Anabaptist Treatise on the Christian and the State," *The Mennonite Quarterly Review*, Jan. 1958, pp. 28-47.

Horsch, John. "Character of the Evangelical Anabaptists," *The Mennonite Quarterly Review*. July, 1934, pp. 123-135.

Horsch, John. "Faith of the Swiss Brethren," *Mennonite Quarterly Review*, Oct. 1930; Jan. 1931; April 1931.

Horsch, John. *Infant Baptism, Its Origin Among Protestants.* Scottdale, Pennsylvania, 1917.

Horsch, John. *Mennonites in Europe.* Scottdale, Pennsylvania: Herald Press, 1950.

Horsch, John. *Menno Simons, His Life, Labors, and Teachings.* Scottdale, Pennsylvania, 1916.

Krahn, Cornelius. *Menno Simons (1496-1561). Ein Beitrag zur Geschichte und Theologie der Taufgesinnten.* Karlsruhe i.B.: Heinrich Schneider, 1936.

Kühler, W. J. *Geschiedenis der Nederlandsche Doopsgezinden.* I, Haarlem, 1932; II, Haarlem, 1940.

Littell, Franklin H. *The Anabaptist View of the Church.* Philadelphia, 1952; second edition, Boston: Starr King Press, Beacon Hill, 1958.

Marbeck, Pilgram. *Antwort auf Kaspar Schwenckfelds Beurteilung des Buches der Bundesbezeugung.* Herausgegeben von J. Loserth, Wien und Leipzig, 1929.

Menno Simons, c. 1496-1561, The Complete Writings of. Translated from the Dutch by Leonard Verduin and edited by John Christian Wenger, with a biography by Harold S. Bender. Scottdale, Pennsylvania: Herald Press, 1956.

Newman, A. H. *A History of Anti-Pedobaptism.* Philadelphia, 1897.

Peachey, Paul. *Die sociale Herkunft der Schweizer Täufer.* Karlsruhe, 1954.

Philip, Dietrich. *Enchiridion or Handbook of the Christian Doctrine and Religion.* Elkhart, Indiana: Mennonite Publishing Co., 1910.

Quellen zur Geschichte der Täufer. Quellen und Forschungen zur Reformationsgeschichte. Herausgegeben vom Verein für Reformationsgeschichte. M. Krebs, *Baden und Pfalz,* 1951; K. Schornbaum, *Bayern,* I, 1934; II, 1951; Krebs und Rott, *Elsass,* I, 1959; II, 1960; Köhler, Sohm, und Sippell, *Hesse,* 1951; L. Müller, *Oberdeutscher Taufgesinner,* 1938; Von Muralt und Schmid, *Schweiz,* 1952; G. Bossert, *Württemberg,* 1930.

Rideman, Peter. *Account of Our Religion, Doctrine and Faith* [1545]. Hodder and Stoughton, Ltd., 1950.

Sattler, Michael. "The Schleitheim Confession of Faith," *The Mennonite Quarterly Review.* Oct., 1945, pp. 243-253.

Sattler, Michael. "Concerning the Satisfaction of Christ," *Mennonite Quarterly Review.* Oct. 1946, pp. 243-254.

Sattler, Michael. "Two Kinds of Obedience," *Mennonite Quarterly Review.* Jan., 1947, pp. 18-22.

Schraepler, Horst W., Dr. Jur. *Die Rechtliche Behandlung der Täufer in der deutschen Schweiz, Südwestdeutschland und Hessen, 1525-1618.* Bearbeitet von Ekkehart Fabian, Tübingen, 1957.

Schreiber, William I. *The Fate of the Prussian Mennonites.* Göttingen, 1955.

Smith, C. Henry. *The Story of the Mennonites.* Revised and enlarged by Cornelius Krahn. Newton, Kansas: Mennonite Publication Office, 1950.

Smithson, R. J. *The Anabaptists, Their Contribution to Our Protestant Heritage.* London: James Clarke & Co., 1935.

Torbet, Robert G. *A History of the Baptists.* Philadelphia: The Judson Press, 1950.

Van Braght, Thieleman J. *The Bloody Theater or Martyrs Mirror.* Scottdale, Pennsylvania: Mennonite Publishing House, 1950. Translated from the Dutch edition of 1660 by Joseph F. Sohm (1855-1902). 1,157 pages.

Van der Zijpp, N. *Geschiedenis der Doopsgezinden in Nederland.* Arnheim: Van Loghum Slaterus, 1952.

Vedder, Henry C. *Balthasar Hübmaier, The Leader of the Anabaptists.* New York and London: G. P. Putnam's Sons, 1905.

Von Muralt, Leonhard. *Glaube und Lehre der Schweizerischen Wiedertäufer in der Reformationszeit.* Zurich, 1938.

Vos, K. *Menno Simons, 1496-1561. Zijn Leven en Werken en Zijne Reformatorische Denkbeelden.* Leiden: E. J. Brill, 1914.

Wenger, John C. *Glimpses of Mennonite History and Doctrine.* Scottdale, Pennsylvania: Herald Press, third edition, 1959.

Williams, George Huntston, and Mergal, Angel M. *Spiritual and Anabaptist Writers.* Volume XXV, *The Library of Christian Classics.* Philadelphia: The Westminster Press, 1957.

Zieglschmid, A. J. F. *Die älteste Chronik der Hutterischen Brüder.* Philadelphia: The Carl Schurz Memorial Foundation, Inc., 1943.

Zieglschmid, A. J. F. *Das Klein-Geschichtsbuch der Hutterischen Brüder.* Philadelphia: The Carl Schurz Memorial Foundation, Inc., 1947.